GARNISHMENT

FOR

WASHINGTON EMPLOYERS

A Practical Guide to Garnishment
Practice, Procedure, and Issues

JEFF SMOOT

Washington Garnishment Procedure: A Practical Guide to Garnishment Practice, Procedure, and Issues

First Edition

Published by 601 Associates LLC, Seattle, Washington

ISBN: 9781790489619

Title 27, Revised Code of Washington (Appendix 7) is public domain.

All photos by the author.

DISCLAIMER

CONTENTS

GARNISHMENT

"A Writ of Garnishment is not to be trifled with, as many a layman has found, to his cost. It can only be prudently dealt with by going to the expense of employing an attorney."

Knettle v. Kennett, 12 Wn.2d 261 (1942)

SUPERIOR COURT OF WASHINGTON
COUNTY OF KING

NO. 11-2-12345-6 XYZ

FRIENDLY FINANCE COMPANY,
      Plaintiff,

vs.

RICK SMITH,
      Defendant(s),

YOUR COMPANY,
      Garnishee.

FIRST ANSWER TO WRIT OF
GARNISHMENT FOR
CONTINUING LIEN ON
EARNINGS
(ANWRGR)

SECTION I: If you are withholding the defendant's nonexempt earnings unde_____ viously
served writ for a continuing lien, answer only sections I and III of this form _____ l or deliver
the forms as directed in the writ. Withhold from the defendant's future n_____ pt earnings as
directed in the writ, and a second set of answer forms will be forwarde_____ later.

If you are NOT withholding the defendant's earnings under a pre_____ served writ for a
continuing lien, answer this ENTIRE form and mail or deliver t_____ s as directed in the writ
second set of answer forms will be forwarded to you later f_____ quently withheld earnings

ANSWER: I am presently holding the defendant's non_____ earnings under a previous wri
served on _____ (date) that will termina_____ ater than _____
(date).

On the date the Writ of Garnishment was_____ dicated by the date appearing on the
page of the writ,

(A) The defendant: (check one) ☐ _____ ☐ vas not employed by garnishee. If not emplo
and you have no possession or _____ ny funds of defendant, indicate the last day of
employment:_____ mplete section III of this answer and mail or delive
forms as directed in the w_____

(B) The defendant: (chec_____ ☐ did ☒ did not maintain a financial account with garni
and

_____ ☒ did ☐ did not have possession of or control over an

INTRODUCTION

Experience is a great teacher. However, it is usually the experience of screwing up something that teaches us the most about it. While most mistakes are eventually rectified, mistakes made while dealing with writs of garnishment teach us a valuable lesson: it is all too easy to screw up a writ of garnishment. There are so many nuances in the garnishment statute—"magic words" that have to be included in the writ, notices that must be provided, short deadlines that cannot be missed—that one must not trifle with a writ of garnishment, but must take it seriously.

Over the years, I have often received phone calls from bewildered employers who, having been served with a writ of garnishment demanding that they withhold earnings from an employee, are mystified by the process. They have read the writ of garnishment, but it is so wordy and technical that they still have no idea what to do. Garnishment forms have been simplified over the years, but it can still a daunting task.

Given the frequency of calls from employers trying to understand the garnishment process so they can correctly fill out an answer form, send it in, and withhold earnings from an employee, I wrote a short article for a local publication explaining the process. Over the years, that article mushroomed into a book-length primer on garnishment procedure for employers, which I have published here in the hope that it will be of assistance to some poor payroll clerk, controller, or small business owner who has been assigned the unenviable task of processing garnishments, a thankless job if ever there was one.

1.

DEFINING "GARNISHMENT"

To many employers, garnishment is a mysterious and confusing procedure. Yet garnishment is really no more mysterious than any other payroll deduction, and once understood will create no more confusion than employee income tax withholding. What probably makes garnishment so widely misunderstood, even feared by employers, is that most employers rarely have to deal with garnishment. Unless you have thousands of employees, like Boeing, Microsoft, Weyerhaeuser, or Alaska Airlines, garnishments may be few and far between, whereas with income tax withholding, even if you have only two employees, you have to deal with it at every payroll period. Large corporations may receive dozens of garnishments every day and have a payroll clerk or two whose primary job is to respond to writs of garnishment and child support withholding orders. But for many small businesses, a wage garnishment might come along only once or twice a decade, if that often.

If you own or manage a small or medium-sized business with only a few employees, you might think it doesn't matter if you don't completely understand the garnishment procedure because you're rarely going to have to deal with a writ of garnishment. Unfortunately, unfamiliarity with garnishment procedure can be very costly. Ask someone who has incorrectly responded to a writ of garnishment. Like other laws, ignorance of garnishment law is not a defense.

Garnishment is simply a statutory means for a judgment creditor to force a third party to withhold money or property owed to a judgment debtor so it may be applied to the satisfaction of a judgment debt. Garnishments are effective against all kinds of property rights, but are most-commonly used to enforce satisfaction of judgments against three kinds of property: wages, bank accounts, and debts due.

In the employment context, think of a writ of garnishment as a court order directing you, the employer, to withhold a percentage of your employee's earnings and pay the withheld money over to a creditor.

Simple enough? Not really. Unfortunately, Washington's garnishment statutes and forms are sometimes difficult to comprehend. Don't worry! Many lawyers have trouble understanding garnishment procedure completely.

Here are some real-life examples of what can happen if you don't properly respond to a garnishment. The names have been changed to protect the ignorant.

> ABC Company was served with a Writ of Garnishment which directed it to withhold wages from Debbie Debtor. The payroll clerk could find no record of Debbie Debtor having ever been an employee, so he didn't respond and forgot about the garnishment. Unfortunately, because ABC did not answer the writ within twenty days as required by law, the creditor's attorney obtained a default judgment against ABC for the full amount of the judgment owed by Debbie, then garnished ABC's payroll account on the first of the following month. Even though ABC had never employed Debbie, it got stuck with the judgment for failing to answer the writ.

XYZ Corporation was served with a Writ of Garnishment against a current employee, Danny Deadbeat. The payroll clerk called the creditor's attorney for help. The attorney told the clerk just to mail in 25% of Danny's wages until the judgment was paid, so the payroll clerk did so, mailing in 25% of gross wages for almost a year, despite Danny's protest that the writ was only good for sixty days, until the full amount stated in the Writ was paid. A month later, Danny filed a lawsuit against the business, claiming it had improperly withheld wages, asking for twice the amount wrongfully withheld plus attorney's fees, as allowed by statute.

Mega Corporation was served with a wage garnishment while its payroll clerk was on vacation. The paperwork was put in her in-basket, where she found it two weeks later. Meanwhile, the employee had retired, and Mega Corporation had paid him an early retirement "bonus" of $10,000. The payroll clerk answered that the employee was no longer employed by Mega Corporation, and no earnings were being withheld. The judgment creditor "controverted" the answer, and subpoenaed the company's payroll records, by which it discovered the bonus payments made after the writ was served. Mega Corporation ended up having to pay the judgment creditor several thousand dollars, plus attorney's fees and costs.

Garnishment horror stories are plentiful, but the cause of the problem is usually the same: The employer didn't understand the process, and the creditor's attorney did. It is hoped that these materials will give you a better understanding of the process, so you don't ever have your own garnishment horror story to tell.

2.

GARNISHMENT PROCEDURE

In order to understand how garnishment works, follow this hypothetical: Your employee, Rick Smith, borrowed money from Friendly Finance Company, but couldn't repay the loan. Friendly Finance eventually sued Rick and got a judgment against him for $5,000. Friendly Finance then applied to the court clerk for issuance of a Writ of Garnishment directing Your Company, as Rick's employer, to withhold money from Rick's wages. The clerk issued the Writ (Appendix 1), which was served on your payroll clerk this morning. Now what?

A. WRIT OF GARNISHMENT

Again, think of a Writ of Garnishment as a court order requiring you to withhold money from your employee's wages. That part is easy enough for most employers to figure out without the help of a lawyer. What is not so easy is figuring out what the writ is telling you to do—that is, how much are you supposed to withhold, how often, for how long, and what are you supposed to do with the money after you withhold it?

ISSUANCE OF A WRIT OF GARNISHMENT

After a judgment debtor fails to voluntarily pay a judgment (which happens most of the time), the judgment creditor may apply to the court clerk for issuance of a Writ of Garnishment. The clerk will issue a Writ of Garnishment without prior notice to you or your employee. The only requirements are that your employee has an unsatisfied judgment against him, and that the judgment creditor has a good-faith belief you are his employer or are indebted to the him in amounts exceeding allowed exemptions. RCW 6.27.060(3) and (4). (Exemptions will be explained later.)

(In district court cases, the judgment creditor's attorney can self-issue a Writ of Garnishment; in superior court cases, the court clerk has to issue the writ.)

Unfortunately, the court clerk will issue a Writ of Garnishment naming you as the "garnishee defendant" (the party being charged with answering the writ and withholding funds) even if you in fact are not now and never have been the judgment debtor's employer. And the writ may be issued without prior notice to anybody.

The effect of a Writ of Garnishment naming you as a garnishee defendant is that you have, without your knowledge, become a party to a lawsuit. As such, you should defend yourself by properly answering the writ in a timely fashion and consulting your attorney if you have any questions about the process.

As a matter of public policy, the Washington Legislature has recognized that a garnishee defendant has no responsibility for the situation leading to the garnishment of a debtor's wages, funds, or other property. RCW 6.27.005. Therefore, when interpreting the garnishment statutes, courts will generally apply the statutes more liberally in favor of the garnishee defendant—who is in effect an innocent bystander caught up in the garnishment proceeding—and more strictly against the judgment creditor.

The courts normally protect garnishee defendants by requiring that the creditor strictly comply with all statutory procedures governing garnishment. *Bartel v. Zucktriegel*, 112 Wn. App. 55, 66, 47 P.3d 581 (2002) (citing *Watkins v. Peterson Enters., Inc.*, 137 Wn.2d 632, 640, 973 P.2d 1037 (1999)). Thus, if the judgment creditor does anything incorrectly or improperly in issuing or serving the Writ of Garnishment, the court will usually invalidate the writ or at least not enforce it against an unsuspecting employer or other garnishee defendant.

DIFFERENT TYPES OF GARNISHMENT

There are several types of garnishments—or, more correctly, there are several types of property which judgment creditors may garnish, including wages or earnings, bank accounts, debts due, and personal property.

A Writ of Garnishment can be effective against all of the following types of property, and more:

- Cash

- Bonuses

- Accrued vacation pay

- Loan payments due

- Contract payments due

- Lease or rent payments due

- Certificates of deposit

- Funds held in trust/escrow accounts

- Contents of safe deposit boxes

- Inventory and equipment held for the debtor

A Writ of Garnishment may direct a garnishee to freeze a judgment debtor's accounts and pay over all funds held by the garnishee on behalf of that judgment debtor; or it may direct a third person to pay a debt due to the judgment debtor to the judgment creditor instead. So if you are holding any property that belongs to the employee, or are owed any money by the employee, it may be subject to the Writ of Garnishment. When in doubt, ask an attorney who understands garnishment procedure.

As an employer, you would ordinarily encounter wage garnishments, those which direct you to withhold a percentage of an employee's earnings. However, it is important to recognize the broad reach of a Writ of Garnishment, and to be aware of the many types of property which are subject to garnishment. Just because the Writ of Garnishment says it is for earnings, it may also apply to any other type of funds or property belonging to or being held for the employee.

B. WAGE GARNISHMENT—"CONTINUING LIEN ON EARNINGS"

In the case of a wage garnishment, the Writ of Garnishment imposes a "continuing lien on earnings" directing the employer to withhold a percentage of the employee's wages or earnings each pay period for a certain length of time. RCW 6.27.330.

Under Washington law, up to 25% of an employee's net pay may be withheld each pay period (up to 60% if the garnishment is for child support) for a period of sixty days after the date of service of the writ, or until the full amount of the judgment is withheld, whichever occurs sooner.

As defined in Washington's garnishment statute, "earnings" include all wages, salary, bonuses, commissions, and any other income earned by the employee for personal services (including contract employee payments). RCW 6.27.010(1).

The term "disposable earnings" refers to earnings remaining after deduction of all amounts <u>required</u> by law to be withheld. RCW 6.27.010(2). (More about required deductions later.)

Under a wage garnishment (also called a "continuing lien on earnings" garnishment), you must withhold the appropriate percentage from <u>all</u> earnings of your employee, whether or not your employee is paid on an hourly, commission, contract, or salary basis.

As an example, in our hypothetical employee Rick's case, Friendly Finance's Writ of Garnishment for Continuing Lien on Earnings directs you to withhold 25% of Rick's net wages for the next sixty days, or until the original $5,000 judgment, plus interest, garnishment costs, and attorney's fees, is paid in full. The writ is served on April 1st; thus, it is effective through the last payday to fall within sixty days after April 1st.

As a general rule, you don't count the date of service in the calculation of deadlines following service. However, because the "effective date" of a Writ of Garnishment is the date of service, you are required to start withholding on the date you receive the garnishment. Therefore, in the case of a garnishment, a common interpretation of the statute is that time begins to run from the date of service.

My interpretation is that because the statute says the employer is to withhold through the last payroll period that falls "on or before sixty days <u>after</u> the effective date of the writ" (emphasis added), you do not count the date of service in your calculation of the sixty days. Thus, if the writ was served on April 1st and there was a payroll period on May 31st, you would have to withhold on May 31st, but continue withholding until the last pay period that occurs up to and including July 30th.

The only time that this will be a problematic issue is if the day in question—either the service date or the last day of the sixty-day period—is a payday. In this situation, it becomes critically important to know whether the sixty days includes the effective date. If the calculation of sixty days "after" the effective date means that the sixty days does not include the effective date, then you would have to withhold from the earnings paid on what is effectively "day 61" after the date of service. But if the sixty days includes the effective date, you don't.

If this situation arises in a garnishment you are dealing with, you should ask your attorney for advice, as opinions may differ as to when the sixty-day effective period of a wage garnishment expires.

Assuming in our example that Rick's garnishment is served on April 1st, and you pay Rick $5,000 gross salary each month and withhold $1,000 for taxes and such, leaving $4,000 net salary payable to Rick each month. Rick is paid $2,000 net salary twice each month (semi-monthly), on the 15th and the last day of each month. Under this scenario, you would withhold from Rick's wages as follows:

Date	Calculation	Withhold
April 1	Nothing	$0.00
April 15	25% of $2,000	$500
April 30	25% of $2,000	$500
May 15	25% of $2,000	$500
May 31	25% of $2,000	$500
TOTAL WITHHELD:		$2,000

You would not withhold wages on April 1st unless payday was April 1st and you had not already paid Rick at the time the writ was served. (If your attorney advised you that May 31st fell outside the sixty-day effective period of the writ, then you would not withhold for that pay period, at your peril.)

Writs served on paydays may present a problem for many employers, particularly those who have already prepared payroll prior to the actual payday. In practice, if you have already given your employee her paycheck before the writ is served or pay via direct deposit, you need not withhold for that payday because you have already paid the employee and do not owe any wages as of the date of service.

Legally, payment occurs when you tender (i.e., hand over) the employee's paycheck, so you need not put a stop payment on a paycheck already issued to your employee if you are served with a garnishment before the employee negotiates the check. You are deemed to have released your obligation to your employee as soon as you give him or her the paycheck. Once the check is in the employee's hands (or in the mail or direct deposited), you have no further payment obligation to your employee for that payday, and thus no longer have funds to withhold.

However, if you have not yet paid your employee (e.g., given the employee his or her paycheck, mailed it, or made a direct deposit), even though it may be an inconvenience (especially if you use a payroll-processing service such as ADP, Benefit Mall, or PayNorthwest, you must withhold under the writ on that payday.

In that case, pull the employee's paycheck and issue a new one, less the 25% or other applicable withholding amount. If you use a payroll-processing service, you may have to cut a manual check. Again, this may be inconvenient, but it is appropriate to protect you from potential liability for failing to withhold as directed by the Writ of Garnishment.

If all this still isn't clear, don't worry. Withholding under a Writ of Garnishment is discussed in greater detail below. But again, anytime you are not sure what to do, ask your attorney for advice.

EXCEPTIONS TO CONTINUING LIEN

Be sure to read the Writ of Garnishment carefully to make sure it is a "continuing lien on earnings" before you withhold wages from an employee. If the writ does not specifically state "continuing lien on earnings" in the caption, and if the body of the writ does not specifically direct you to withhold earnings (compare examples in Appendix 2-3), it is not a continuing lien and you MUST NOT withhold wages for sixty days.

Further, if the answer form does not list the minimum amounts to be paid to an employee as required by RCW 6.27.340, the employer may treat the writ as one that is not a continuing lien.

In summary, a writ which does not meet the requirements for a continuing lien is deemed an ordinary writ of garnishment, and you would withhold only that money or property of the employee/debtor which you owed or held at the moment the writ was served, or answered, whichever is later. If you withhold wages for sixty days under a writ which is not a continuing lien, you could be liable for wrongful withholding of your employee's wages.

Also, although only "earnings" are subject to the "continuing lien" aspect of the writ, a continuing lien garnishment is effective against not only earnings, but also against any other payments or debts you may owe to the employee as of the date of service, including dividends, note payments, loan repayments, contract payments, reimbursements, and other property.

Simply put, a wage garnishment is effective not only against wages but other property as well; but a non-wage garnishment is not effective against wages—except wages owed at the moment the writ is served.

Assume that, as of April 1st, the date of service of our hypothetical writ, you also owe Rick $250 for some truck parts he sold to the company. You would be required to withhold that money and account for it in your answer, in addition to Rick's earnings.

But let's say later that day, a couple of hours after the writ was served, Rick sold you an additional $500 worth of truck parts. What then? Ordinarily, the writ would not be effective against that $500, even though the continuing lien is still effective against earnings for the following sixty days, because the continuing lien is only effective against earnings, not other debts.

However, if you delay in answering the writ for a few days, you may have to answer that you are withholding $750 in addition to the wages. Also, if another writ was served on you before you paid the $500 to Rick, you would have to withhold that $500 under the second writ, even though a "continuing lien" was still in effect against Rick's earnings.

Confused yet? Just wait.

Here's another example: Assume Your Company is a bank, and Rick is a teller who also has an account at the bank. When the bank is served with the continuing lien on earnings writ, it is required to withhold not only Rick's earnings under the "continuing lien," but is also required to withhold whatever is in Rick's bank account at the moment the writ is served (if the writ also complies with the requirements for garnishing bank accounts). But, if more money is deposited into the account after you have answered the writ, that additional money need not be withheld because it is not earnings subject to the continuing lien.

So if Rick has only $100 in the account at 3:15 p.m. when the writ is served and answered, Friendly Finance gets only that $100 (plus 25% of Rick's earnings for the next sixty days under the continuing lien), even if at 3:30 p.m. Rick deposits another $1,000 into the account. If the writ was not answered until 4 p.m., however, the writ could be effective against the additional $1,000.

As a creditor's attorney, I might argue that it is effective against any funds held at the time the writ is answered. As a debtor's attorney, I might argue the opposite. There would probably be a hearing held to sort out how much should have been withheld. Avoiding this kind of confusion and the litigation that can ensue is one reason why it is important to answer a Writ of Garnishment as soon as possible. The longer you delay answering, the more questions and issues arise and the greater your chances of screwing things up.

Of course, under the "continuing lien," the employee's earnings continue to be withheld for sixty days regardless of any other debts or moneys owed to the employee. But again, a garnishment that is not a "continuing lien" is effective only at the moment of service or answer, whichever is later. (More about this later.)

Also, don't forget that a "continuing lien" writ is effective against earnings only as to *pay periods* which fall within sixty days of the effective date. Unless the payday falls within the sixty days after the effective date, it is not subject to withholding under the writ. Any pay periods which fall outside the sixty-day effective period of the "continuing lien" are not subject to withholding under the writ.

Finally, remember that any payments due which are not "earnings" are not subject to the "continuing lien" aspect of the garnishment, but are withheld only as of the date the writ is served or answered, whichever is later.

C. SERVICE OF THE WRIT

Service of a Writ of Garnishment is the actual delivery of the writ to the garnishee defendant. Service of a Writ of Garnishment may be by personal service to the owner, an officer, or other authorized person in the company, or by certified mail.

A Writ of Garnishment is effective at the moment it is received by you, and **IT MUST BE PROCESSED <u>IMMEDIATELY</u>**.

At the moment of service of a Writ of Garnishment, you must not pay any debts or wages owed to your employee except as provided in the garnishment statutes, or as directed by court order. RCW 6.27.120(1). If you do pay any funds to your employee after service of a Writ of Garnishment, except exempt earnings, you become liable to the judgment creditor for payment of those amounts.

This prohibition does not apply to exempt amounts, which you are required by law to pay to your employee despite the garnishment. Also, if the amount you owe to your employee is more than the amount stated in the writ, you need only withhold the amount stated in the writ, and you may pay the excess to your employee without incurring any liability to the judgment creditor except as to the amount withheld. RCW 6.27.120(2) and (3).

In order for service of a Writ of Garnishment to be effective, you must be served with all of the following documents together at the same time:

> (1) The original Writ of Garnishment (or a copy bearing the court seal and clerk's signature or stamp if issued from a superior court judgment, only the issuing attorney's signature if issued from a district court judgment); and

> (2) A blank answer form.

> [See RCW 6.27.110(1); Appendix 7][1]

---

[1] The former requirement that the writ be accompanied by three blank answer forms and stamped return envelopes has been abolished.

Look carefully at all papers served with the writ to make sure each of these items is received. To be sure, list each document received as soon as you are served (or make a copy of everything you received). If you do not receive each of these items together, service is insufficient. This does not mean you should simply toss the writ in the garbage and forget it, though. Nor does it mean you can refuse service. You should still accept service of the writ, even if service seems defective, and answer the writ as soon as possible by filling out and mailing the answer form (original to the court, copies to everyone else) in the envelopes provided, following the instructions in the writ.

If service appears to be defective, for any reason, you should note any obvious defects in your answer, to put the garnishing creditor on notice, and also so your employee will have a basis for contesting the garnishment.

If service is ineffective because of a judgment creditor's failure to serve all required documents with the writ, you are under no legal obligation to withhold earnings or pay debts owed to your employee. In fact, you may incur liability to your employee if you withhold under an ineffective garnishment. For this reason, you must be absolutely certain service was effective before you withhold earnings from your employee, and you must be certain service was ineffective if you do not withhold under the writ due to invalid service.

In such cases, because it is a legal question whether service was effective, it is wise to ask your attorney to review the papers and advise you as to the validity of service.

You should point out even the smallest service defect in your answer. It used to be that a stamped envelope to the court clerk had to be served with a Writ of Garnishment. If the envelope had the wrong court address on it, defect rendered the writ invalid. Judges have quashed Writs of Garnishment and awarded attorney's fees to the garnishee defendant as a result of this simple error.

Suppose no answer form is included with the writ at the time of service but a few days later you receive a blank answer form in the mail. Does this fix the problem? Definitely not. In order for service to be effective, the writ and blank answer form must be served together. If, however, a few days later you receive a new writ with all of the required attachments, that would cure the defect and you would start withholding from the date of the second service.

It is good practice to make a checklist to make sure you received all necessary documents when you are served with a garnishment, even better practice to copy everything you received and have your attorney or garnishment specialist review them to be sure service was effective.

If you are not sure whether service was valid, you should still begin withholding, but should notify your employee and the garnishing creditor as soon as possible of any perceived defect. By notifying your employee, you put him or her on notice that they can challenge the garnishment, which will reduce or eliminate your liability for improper withholding if service is finally found to be improper.

Either way, you should withhold earnings as directed by the writ and not pay them over to the garnishing creditor until ordered to do so by the court. This way, if the employer successfully challenges service, you can pay the withheld earnings to the employee after the court decides and avoid potential liability for wrongful withholding of wages. Likewise, if the challenge to service is unsuccessful, you can pay the withheld earnings to the garnishing creditor.

WHO MAY BE SERVED?

As noted previously, service of a Writ of Garnishment may be by personal service or certified mail. Personal service of a Writ of Garnishment must be made upon certain persons to be valid, depending upon what type of business you operate:

Sole Proprietorships: Service must be on the owner, or the business manager, to be effective. As a practical matter, service upon the payroll director is considered valid service. Service on a clerk, receptionist, part-time employee, salesperson, secretary, or any other employee may be ineffective in some cases.

Partnerships: Service must be on the Managing Partner or any General Partner, or the business manager, cashier, controller, payroll director; but not on a clerk, receptionist, part-time employee, secretary, salesperson, or any other employee.

Corporations: Service may be on the President, Secretary, Manager, Cashier, Registered Agent, or the personal secretary of any of these, or the payroll clerk or another designated person or agent; but, again, usually not a clerk, receptionist, part-time employee, secretary, salesperson or any other employee, except as noted above.

An owner, officer, or registered agent may be served at home. Service on anyone "of suitable age and discretion" at the owner, officer, or registered agent's home may be effective service on the company. All others must be served at the place of business.

Service on a janitor is not good service, but service on the receptionist may be effective service, particularly if the receptionist's job duties include receiving incoming documents and deliveries. At least, the judgment creditor will argue that service was effective.

You should not quibble over service defects relating to the authority of the person served to receive legal process, unless the person served is clearly not a person upon whom service may be made. But if you have any questions about effectiveness of service, ask your attorney for advice.

SERVICE BY CERTIFIED MAIL

Service by certified mail is effective if mailed to your business address or post office box, no matter who signs for it, and it is deemed effective immediately as of the date the receipt is signed (a really good reason for opening all certified mail immediately!). Thus, if you receive a garnishment in the mail but fail to act upon it quickly, your delay may be costly.

It is important to instruct all staff who receive deliveries or open mail to PROMPTLY deliver any garnishment papers to the payroll clerk or appropriate officer IN PERSON so the writ can be dealt with immediately. All too many times, employers get into trouble for not answering writs on time because they are misrouted, misfiled, or put in somebody's in-box while they are on vacation.

EFFECT OF IMPROPER SERVICE

Again, if a Writ of Garnishment is not properly served, it is ineffective. That means, if you withhold wages from an employee based on an improperly served writ, your withholding may be found to be wrongful, and may entitle your employee to recourse against you.

But be careful! If service appears defective and you fail to withhold earnings, but the court decides service was effective, you may be liable to the judgment creditor for amounts you should have withheld under the writ. It is a two-edged sword, so be doubly careful.

What should you do if service appears improper? For starters, even if you suspect the garnishment was improperly served, you should still respond to the writ. NEVER IGNORE A WRIT OF GARNISHMENT! If you have any doubts, consult with your attorney before you make a mistake.

If you can't consult with your attorney, and aren't sure what to do, err on the side of caution and withhold all funds and property subject to the writ, and do not release the withholding until you receive a court order directing you to release the withheld funds or property or until your attorney advises you otherwise. Immediately notify your employee of your withholding, and of the possible service defects, so your employee may independently seek to have the garnishment declared ineffective and to obtain a court order quashing the writ and directing release of the garnished wages.

If your attorney tells you to withhold nothing because service is defective, or if you are able to independently determine whether service was defective, you should not withhold under the writ, and you should answer that you have withheld nothing because service was invalid. (Better yet, have your attorney sign the answer so if it is incorrect, your attorney will have to deal with the consequences.)

In any case, act quickly, since delays in answering the writ may subject you to liability. And again, never, ever ignore a Writ of Garnishment. If you ignore the writ, even though it was improperly served, you may end up paying someone else's attorney's fees as well as your own, or worse!

D.   ANSWERING THE WRIT

When you answer properly, and withhold properly, you discharge your obligation under the writ. When you answer improperly, withhold improperly, or fail to timely answer, you increase your liability under the writ.

As noted above, you should answer a Writ of Garnishment immediately. Delays in answering are the biggest problem encountered by garnishee defendants. Any delay in answering a Writ of Garnishment could be costly.

For example, suppose your mail clerk signed for a garnishment served by certified mail on Friday, and left it in your payroll clerk's in-basket. But your payroll clerk was out sick that Friday and didn't return until Monday, a payday, and she didn't find the garnishment in her in-basket until after lunch because she was busy getting paychecks out. Then suppose you had already given Rick his $2,000 paycheck on Monday morning, along with a $250 check for the truck parts. What just happened?

The effect of failing to answer the writ on Friday and failure to withhold the earnings from Rick's paycheck issued on Monday is that now you, the employer, are liable to Friendly Finance for the $500 you should have withheld from Rick's paycheck and the $250 debt you paid to Rick after service of the writ.

Since the mistake was your fault, you don't have any legal recourse against Rick to recover those amounts. That means you can't make Rick give the money back, and you can't do backup withholding from Rick's next paycheck to make up for what you failed to withhold from this paycheck. (You can, but you may subject yourself to a claim of improper withholding of wages.)

If Rick is cooperative, he might give the money back voluntarily, but he is under no legal obligation to do so. Rick might also agree to allow the writ to be effective for sixty days from the date answered. Or he might work out a payment plan with the creditor and authorize direct payroll deductions.

What usually happens is the employer starts withholding during the next payroll period, and neither the employee or the garnishing creditor notice or care about the delay. While this is not technically the correct approach, it is usually the most expedient solution for the employer.

Remember that your answer must account not only for your employee's wages, but also any other debts owed to or property held for your employee. But what is most important is that you answer the writ as soon as you can, since answering is the first step in discharging your obligation under the writ.

FIRST ANSWER

In the case of a "continuing lien on earnings" garnishment, the judgment creditor must serve a blank answer form—one that specifically instructs the employer to withhold for sixty days. This "first answer" must be filled out, signed, and mailed to the court, the employee, and the judgment creditor, within twenty days of the date of service.

You may choose to fill out your first answer immediately, that day, and mail it immediately, or wait until the next payday before filling out the answer. However, it is recommended that you answer immediately to discharge any potential obligation for failing to timely answer unless there is some strategic reason to delay answering. The sooner you answer, the less likely you will incur any unnecessary liability under the writ.

If you answer immediately, your answer should confirm that Rick is an employee, and should contain an accounting of Rick's anticipated earnings for the next pay period, and should also contain a statement that you will withhold as directed by the writ for the full sixty days. A sample first answer form is provided at Appendix 4.

In addition to this basic information, it may be useful for Friendly Finance's attorney to know when the next pay period will be, and how big or small Rick's regular paycheck is and what is usual deductions are. In your answer, provide all information Friendly Finance needs to know: customary gross earnings, customary deductions, and projected net earnings.

If you choose to wait until the next pay period to answer, be sure you answer within twenty days of the date of service. This means your answer must be RECEIVED by the court and by the judgment creditor within twenty days. Don't wait until the twentieth day to fill it out and mail it. If you wait, it will be late!

If you fail to answer within twenty days, Washington's garnishment statute allows the judgment creditor to obtain a judgment against YOU for the full amount of the debt owed by your employee! RCW 6.27.200. This means you could end up paying your employee's debt, in full, without any recourse.

The garnishing creditor is required to give you a notice of your failure to answer and provide you with a copy of the motion seeking entry of a judgment against you at least ten days before submitting the motion to the court. If you answer within ten days of receiving this notice, all is well. If you happen to miss the ten-day notice, a judgment will be entered against you and you could be stuck paying the entire judgment.

It is recommended that you answer immediately to avoid this problem. By waiting, you run the risk of answering late. It is best to avoid delay and answer quickly.

HOW TO ANSWER

Filling out the first answer forms requires you to perform a basic accounting of your employee's gross wage, less mandatory deductions, less 75%, which is required to be paid to the employee, with the 25% remainder to be withheld under the writ (or up to 60% if the garnishment is for child support). Because the garnishment forms can be confusing, with many blanks to fill in, it may be easier for you to simply type an accounting to attach to the answer and then write or type "See Attached" on the answer form. Such an accounting might look like this:

Gross Pay:	$2,500
Less Withholding:	(500)
Net Pay:	$2,000
75% Exempt:	(1,500)
25% Withheld:	$ 500

[See Appendix 4 for a sample answer form with attachment.]

If the employee no longer works for you, state that in your answer. In this case, you should have no liability under the writ unless you still owe the departed employee any money (such as severance pay).

If the employee quits or is terminated prior to the date of service of the writ, state the employee's termination date and the date of his last paycheck in your answer.

If the employee is active, but is not owed any wages for any reason, say so in your answer, but be sure to explain why in sufficient detail to satisfy the curiosity of the judgment creditor's attorney, who will ask: Is the employee on leave, disability, or vacation without pay? If so, when did it begin, when is the employee expected to be back on a regular schedule, and what is the source of the employee's income if not from you?

Your answer should be sufficiently detailed to answer any question the judgment creditor's attorney might have. A vague or incomplete answer may result in an annoying phone call, a threatening letter, a subpoena, or a court hearing.

To answer, you may either fill out the answer form, sign it, and make three photocopies. Mail the signed original to the court and a copy to the judgment creditor and your employee at the addresses provided in the writ. Keep the third copy for your records.

Sign the answer form before submitting. The effect of an unsigned answer form is the same as if you failed to answer at all, so BE SURE TO SIGN THE ANSWER!

Also, you should make a note on your copy of the first answer stating the date you mailed it. That way, if questioned, you have something to look back to, to refresh your memory, in case the judgment creditor's attorney claims you never mailed the answer form.

If there is a previous Writ of Garnishment, Wage Assigment, or other withholding order in effect at the time the Writ is served, say so in your answer. Also, provide a copy of the prior garnishment or withholding order, and give the date the prior writ is expected to expire.

Wage assignment orders, OSE notices of payroll deduction, DSHS orders to withhold and deliver, and Internal Revenue Service notices of levy are treated differently than other garnishments; these types of orders are discussed in more detail below.

In your answer, especially if claiming you owe nothing to the employee, try to explain your answer rather than just saying "$-0-" or "No funds." Otherwise, you are inviting the judgment creditor's attorney to serve a subpoena or controvert your answer. It is much easier if you write a few details in your answer to explain why no funds are being withheld, such as, for example:

"Rick is on leave until August 1st."

"Rick has a prior writ in effect through July 1st."

"Rick's earnings are subject to a wage assignment for child support."

SPECIAL SITUATIONS

What if the judgment debtor named in the Writ of Garnishment is not an employee of your company, and as far as you can tell, never has been an employee of your company?

Amazingly, some employers have simply thrown the writ away, thinking "He's not an employee, so I don't have to answer." WRONG!

Even if the person named in the writ never worked for you, you can still end up being liable for payment of the entire underlying judgment if you fail to answer the writ within twenty days! ALWAYS ANSWER A WRIT OF GARNISHMENT AS SOON AS POSSIBLE! Even if it is clearly in error.

In this case, you should answer simply that the person named in the writ is not and never has been an employee, and accordingly you are not withholding any funds.

What if you have two employees named "Rick Smith" but you don't know which one is the "Rick Smith" whose wages you are supposed to withhold? Or what if the writ identifies "Rich Smith" as the judgment creditor, but your employee is named "Rick Smith"?

If the judgment creditor provides a Social Security number, address, or a middle initial, that should answer your question. But in cases where you are not sure of the identity of the judgment debtor, you should proceed as follows:

First, call the judgment creditor's attorney and ask him or her to more specifically identify the judgment debtor. Ask for a last-known address, Social Security number, or middle initial.

If that doesn't work, ask both employees named "Rick Smith" which is the "Rick Smith" who owes money to Friendly Finance. Or, in the case of "Rich Smith," since Rick is a nickname of Richard, you should ask Rick if he is the "Rich Smith" who owes money to Friendly Finance.

If that doesn't work, you would begin withholding from both employees named Rick Smith, or from your employee Rick Smith in the case of the garnishment directed to "Rich Smith," and you would state the following in your answer:

> We are indebted to or have possession of personal effects belonging to a person with a name the same as or similar to the name of the defendant, whose address is 1234 Main Street, Anytown USA, but we do not know whether or not that person is the same person as the defendant. We therefore ask the court to determine whether or not the person is the same person as the defendant.

Chances are, once you begin withholding from both employees named "Rick Smith," the one who is not the judgment debtor will so inform you, angrily no doubt. Or in the case of "Rich Smith," the employee named Rick Smith will likewise get upset that you are withholding his wages if he is not the judgment debtor.

If the real Rick Smith or Rich Smith does not make himself known, the court will hold a hearing to determine whether your "Rick Smith" or "Rich Smith" is the same person as the defendant named in the Writ of Garnishment. After the hearing, the court will order you to either (1) release the earnings withheld to your employee who is not the person named in the writ, or (2) release the earnings to the judgment creditor because your employee is the person named in the writ.

In cases where your employee is not the person named in the writ, you will be released from the garnishment, and may even recover costs and attorney's fees from the judgment creditor. In cases where your employee is the person named in the writ, you will be required to pay over the withheld earnings. If you have failed to withhold earnings, you will be liable for the amount you should have withheld.

In cases where the identity of the judgment debtor cannot reasonably be determined, by following the above procedure, you will not be liable to your employee(s) for wrongful withholding of wages, even if it turns out your employee is not the person named in the writ. However, in such cases, because of the potential liability for doing it wrong, it is wise to ask your attorney for advice before answering and withholding.

SECOND ANSWER

Close to the end of the sixty-day effective period of the wage garnishment, you should receive a "second answer" form, along with three more stamped, addressed envelopes. These may be delivered by regular mail, and need not be personally served or certified mailed.

Like the first answer, your second answer is also due within twenty days of the date you receive it, but should not be mailed until the last payday during the sixty days or at the end of the sixty-day period, whichever is first. So, even if the answer is due before the end of the sixty days, but the last payday is more than twenty days from the day you receive the second answer forms, it may be wise to notify the creditor's attorney that you will be holding the second answer until the end of the sixty days before answering.

If you do not file the second answer within the twenty days, the creditor's attorney is required to notify you before requesting a default judgment, assuming you filed the first answer. If the attorney obtains a default judgment against you without notice based on your failure to timely file the second answer, he or she might be liable for your attorney's fees and costs incurred in having the default set aside.

The purpose of the first answer is to inform the court, the judgment creditor, and your employee that you are withholding earnings under the writ. The second answer is to inform the court, the judgment creditor, and your employee of the full amount you have withheld under the Writ of Garnishment during the entire sixty-day effective period of the writ.

Once the judgment creditor's attorney receives your second answer, he or she prepares a "judgment on answer of garnishee defendant" (an "order to pay") and obtains a court order directing you to pay the funds withheld to the clerk of the court. You should not pay any money directly to the creditor until you receive the court's order to pay.

E.   WITHHOLDING UNDER A WRIT OF GARNISHMENT

Withholding under a Writ of Garnishment can be the most confusing part of the process, but it needn't be. It is as easy as calculating employee income tax withholding, but you wouldn't know it from reading the instructions in the writ or the answer form. The most current version of the official state garnishment answer form is fairly straightforward to fill out, but not all attorneys are using the updated form. If you can't understand the instructions in the writ and answer, ignore them. There is an easier way to figure it out:

If the garnishment is not for child support, withhold 25% of the employee's non-exempt wages; if the garnishment is for child support, you may withhold up to 60% of the employee's non-exempt wages. Follow the instructions in the writ.

"Non-exempt wages" are those earnings left over after MANDATORY deductions. "Mandatory deductions" are those required by law to be deducted from your employee's paycheck. They include federal withholding, FICA, Social Security, union dues, and other related deductions, but only those required by law or under the terms of employment to be withheld.

Specifically, mandatory deductions DO NOT include: optional medical insurance, credit union draws, voluntary wage assignments, retirement plan contributions, 401(k) loan repayments, or any other deduction which is taken at the employee's option.

An easy test is: "Could the employee choose not to have this amount deducted?" If the answer is yes, then it is not a mandatory deduction.

Also, despite what many creditor attorneys will tell you, mandatory deductions DO NOT INCLUDE the following: IRS levies, OSE payroll deductions, child support garnishments, or wage assignments to other creditors, even those issued under court order. Although the employee may not simply choose to stop these deductions, they are treated differently than mandatory deductions because they are themselves types of wage garnishments or levies which already affect the employee's non-exempt earnings. These types of wage garnishments are discussed in more detail below.

Say your employee, Rick, earns $2,500 gross per paycheck, from which you deduct $500 federal withholding and $100 for Rick's 401(k) contribution. Rick's non-exempt wages would be $2,000, not $1,900, because only the federal withholding is a mandatory deduction. Rick could elect not to make the $100 401(k) contribution, so that is not a mandatory deduction. Accordingly, you would withhold 25% of $2,000, or $500 per pay period for a period of sixty days.

WRIT SERVED ON PAYDAY

Another question which frequently comes up is: If we have already issued the paycheck when the writ was served, do we need to withhold for this pay period? The answer is: maybe, maybe not.

Assume you were served with the writ on the day before payday. Because the writ is effective from the moment of service, you must withhold from the next day's paycheck. This may be a hassle, especially if the payroll checks have already been printed and signed, but if you don't withhold, you may end up paying what you should have withheld from that paycheck. Accordingly, you should pull that employee's paycheck and issue a new one—minus the withholding, of course.

The problem is amplified when a writ is served on payday. In that case, withholding depends on whether you have or have not paid your employee. A simple test is: Have you already given your employee his or her paycheck? If so, you would not withhold for that payday. If not, you are obligated to withhold from that paycheck.

SIXTY-DAY EFFECTIVE PERIOD

As discussed above, a Writ of Garnishment is effective against all pay periods which fall within the sixty days including and after the date of service.

If the Writ was served the day before a payday, it includes that payday and any paydays which fall with the sixty days after service. If the sixty days ends the day before a payday, because the Writ is effective only as to paydays falling *within* the sixty days after the effective date, you should not withhold from a paycheck issued on day 61 or later, even if some or all of those wages were earned during the preceding sixty days. You also would not withhold a pro-rata portion of wages earned right up to the end of the sixty days; only withhold from regular paychecks or any earnings paid during the sixty days.

To count the sixty days, do not count the effective date. If "E" is the effective date, count E + 60 days to determine the last day the writ is effective.

NEXT STEPS

Although calculating withholding may not be too difficult, you may have trouble figuring out what to do next. After you have withheld the earnings under the writ, what do you do with them? Some employers write a check payable to the judgment creditor each payday, in the amount withheld, and hold those checks aside until told what to do with them, or mail them to the judgment creditor each payday. Others set the withheld earnings aside in a separate account. Others simply hold them in their payroll account, awaiting instructions.

It is recommended that you hold the funds in suspense rather than writing checks to the judgment creditor each pay period. That way, if your account earns interest, you earn interest on the funds while they are being withheld. And you only have to issue one check.

In any case, you should continue holding the withheld funds until you receive a court order directing you to release the funds. Despite what the judgment creditor's lawyer may tell you to do, DO NOT release any of withheld funds to the judgment creditor, its attorney, or the court, until you receive a court order telling you to do so.

The only exception to this rule is if the Writ of Garnishment directs you to make direct payments to the creditor's attorney, you may do so without penalty. Read the writ carefully before proceeding.

If you release any withheld funds without a court order or contrary to the instructions in the writ, you may be liable to your employee for wrongful withholding, particularly if the employee is able to have the garnishment quashed or modified, or if the employee asserts an exemption claim.

PROCESSING FEES

The garnishment statute allows employers to deduct a processing fee of $20 for the first answer and $10 for the second answer from the employee's earnings. This is voluntary on the employer's part, and is taken from the remainder of the employee's earnings after withholding under the writ.

F.   JUDGMENT ON ANSWER

Assuming all goes according to schedule, within a few weeks after you mail in your second answer, you should receive a "Judgment on Answer and Order to Pay." This is a court order requiring you to pay the withheld wages to the clerk of the court (or to the creditor's attorney if the garnishment was issued from district court).

A few things to know about a judgment on answer:

(1)   You should send the money to the court, not to the creditor or its attorney (unless the order directs you to do so as this is allowed in district court garnishments but not in superior court);

(2)   You should send in the amount stated in the judgment, not more, not less; and

(3)   You should comply as soon as possible, because the order to pay is like a judgment: if you don't comply right away, the creditor's attorney can garnish YOU to recover money you were ordered to pay.

When paying withheld funds pursuant to a judgment on answer, make your check payable to the court clerk if directed to pay to the court registry, and reference your employee's name and the court case number on your check. Then either mail or personally deliver the check to the court clerk.

If the order says pay the plaintiff or plaintiff's attorney directly, make the check payable to the plaintiff or attorney and mail it as directed by the order.

Once you deliver the funds pursuant to the order to pay, you have discharged your obligation under the Writ of Garnishment.

3.

COMMON ISSUES AND HOW TO AVOID THEM

Ideally, the garnishment process will go smoothly from start to finish. You will be properly served with all required forms; you will answer on time; you will withhold 25% of your employee's net earnings for sixty days; you will receive a judgment on answer; you will pay the withheld funds to the court clerk; and your obligation under the writ will be discharged.

Unfortunately, there are many situations that commonly arise during the garnishment process. Knowing what to do in these situations is critical to avoiding the many pitfalls of garnishment, avoiding potential liability to your employee and the judgment creditor, and avoiding paying attorney's fees to get yourself out of trouble if you make a mistake.

A. PRIOR WRIT IN EFFECT

What if you are served with a garnishment while you already have a garnishment in effect? Some employers have assumed that the second garnishment is automatically superseded by the first, and have tossed the second garnishment. Big mistake!

Others have answered that, because there was already a garnishment in effect, no funds were withheld. Another mistake!

Think of successive garnishments as cars on a train; they line up behind each other and each is loaded one after the other. Each successive "continuing lien" garnishment is entitled to a full sixty-day withholding period, which begins immediately after the previous garnishment has expired. Writs of Garnishment are polite: they take turns.

Except, that is, for garnishments issued in the same case. If you receive successive garnishments from the same case, they do not automatically have priority over garnishments from other creditors. If another garnishment is served between effective dates of two same-case writs, it has priority over garnishments from the same case—except the writ that is currently in effect.

In Rick's case, assume one garnishment was served on April 1st, and another (from a different creditor) was served on April 2nd. The first writ is effective for sixty days, or until May 31st. The second writ is also effective for sixty days, but that sixty-day period begins on June 1st, after the first garnishment's sixty days has run. And if a third garnishment was served on April 3rd, that writ would also be effective for sixty days, beginning August 1st. And so on, and so on.

When multiple garnishments are served on the same day, the garnishment served first is effective first. The old rule, "first in time, first in right" applies to garnishments. So a garnishment served at 10 a.m. has priority over another garnishment served at 10:05 a.m. Because of this, noting the time of receipt of the Writ of Garnishment is good practice.

What if more than one garnishment is received at the same time, such as by certified mail? In that case, the garnishments take priority in the order you answer them. To protect yourself and avoid arguments about which writ has priority, make a note of the date and time each writ was received and when you sign the answer form.

A creditor may try to "stack" writs of garnishment by having several writs issued simultaneously and serving them all, in the belief that this will shut out other creditors. However, stacking of successive writs issued under the same case number is not allowed; only one writ at a time is valid. If another creditor serves a writ, it would have next priority over a stacked writ.

B.   MULTIPLE GARNISHMENTS AGAINST ONE EMPLOYEE

If your employee's wages are garnished, you may be tempted to terminate that employee, either because the employee's failure to pay his debts is deemed unacceptable, or just to avoid the hassle of dealing with the garnishment. Resist that temptation!

Washington law forbids firing an employee just because his or her wages are garnished. RCW 6.27.170. If you fire an employee because his or her wages are garnished, you might end up defending a wrongful-termination lawsuit.

However, in one of the examples given above, where Rick's wages were garnished by three separate judgment creditors in a very short period, you would be justified in firing Rick. Washington law permits you to terminate an employee if his or her wages are garnished by three or more separate judgment creditors during any consecutive 12-month period. RCW 6.27.170.

Regardless, you may still terminate your employee for other valid reasons, just not because of a garnishment by itself, except under the above circumstances. So if you were already planning on firing your employee, and he or she is garnished before he or she is actually terminated, you can still go ahead and terminate the employee. Just make sure your reasons for the termination are adequately documented so the employee cannot claim you fired him or her just because of the garnishment. You don't need a wrongful termination lawsuit if you can avoid it.

C. CHILD SUPPORT GARNISHMENTS

As previously discussed, if a garnishment is based on child support, up to 60% of your employee's non-exempt earnings may be withheld under the writ, since your employee would be allowed only a 40% exemption (or 50%, depending upon whether he or she is supporting another family and asserts an exemption claim). Of course, the employee still must be paid the federal minimum amounts, no matter what kind of garnishment you are dealing with. A garnishment for child support must still state "continuing lien on earnings" to be valid for sixty days; otherwise, it is a one-shot deal.

Fortunately, actual garnishments for child support are rare. More common are wage assignment orders and notices of payroll deduction. In cases of child support debts (and debts for spousal maintenance), the court may issue a "Voluntary Wage Assignment" or "Mandatory Wage Assignment," which would direct you, the employer, to withhold a certain amount or percentage of your employee's wages (up to 50%) each pay period, and to pay the withheld earnings either to a support registry or directly to the party entitled to payment. These orders usually direct the employer to continue withholding indefinitely, or until a certain amount is paid. In most cases, you should continue withholding the ordered amount until you receive an order telling you to stop, or until your employee no longer works for you. You are usually required also to notify the court when the employee quits or is terminated.

Garnishments for child support have priority over almost any other kind of garnishment. RCW 6.27.360(2). Even the IRS cannot usurp priority over a child support garnishment. Accordingly, if you receive a court-ordered wage assignment or other garnishment for child support while you are already withholding under another garnishment of lesser priority, you should stop withholding under the first garnishment and start withholding under the wage assignment—unless the garnishment in effect is for child support, in which case you should continue withholding under the first garnishment and state in the answer to the second child support garnishment that you already have a child-support garnishment pending.

The only type of garnishment entitled priority over a child support garnishment or wage assignment order is a "notice of payroll deduction" issued by the Office of Support Enforcement. A notice of payroll deduction from the OSE has priority over "any wage assignment, garnishment, attachment, or other legal process." RCW 26.23.060(4). If you receive one, stop withholding under any other garnishment, and notify the garnishing creditor of the reason why withholding has been suspended.

Another type of support order you may receive is an "order to withhold and deliver" from the Department of Social and Health Services. These public assistance orders are usually to collect welfare payments for child support from "deadbeat" parents. Like OSE notices of payroll deduction, orders to withhold and deliver are entitled to priority over all other garnishments—except OSE orders.

D. IRS NOTICE OF LEVY

Similar to an OSE "notice of payroll deduction" is an Internal Revenue Service "notice of levy." An IRS notice will direct you to withhold a certain amount from your employee's wages, or up to 50% of your employee's net earnings. An IRS notice should be treated just like a wage assignment order or OSE notice, since it has priority over other garnishments, except garnishments for child support.

Again, trouble arises when you have a pending IRS levy and you are served with another garnishment. Treat this situation just like you would an OSE notice or wage assignment order: if the other garnishment is for child support or spousal support, stop withholding and notify the IRS; otherwise, keep withholding and notify the other creditor of the IRS levy.

However, it may be appropriate to withhold under both an OSE or IRS levy and a lower-priority writ of garnishment. This is discussed in more detail below. When in doubt, call your attorney.

E. PRIORITY OF COMPETING WRITS

Generally, wage garnishments, wage assignments, and other wage levies should be given the following priority:

1. OSE notice of payroll deduction (administrative order);

2. Public Assistance notice of payroll deduction (administrative order);

3. Tie between:

   - Mandatory wage assignment for child support or spousal maintenance (court order);

   - Voluntary wage assignment for child support or spousal maintenance (court order);

   - Writ of Garnishment for child support (court issued);

4. IRS levy (administrative order);

5. Writ of Garnishment (issued pursuant to RCW 6.27);

6. Voluntary wage assignment (not for child support).

This list is generally an accurate guide to garnishment priorities. But if you ever find yourself with conflicting wage withholding orders and garnishments for child support, spousal maintenance, public assistance, and/or tax levies, it is a good idea to call your attorney for advice. The likelihood is that one or the other of the garnishing creditors will claim to have priority over the other, meaning a court hearing or some negotiation may be necessary.

In any case, withhold the maximum amount directed under each conflicting levy until you receive a court order telling you what to do.

One common misconception among employers and attorneys is that, once an OSE notice of payroll deduction, wage assignment, or IRS levy is in effect, it renders all other garnishments ineffective. Although usually that is the case, it is not automatically true.

Since wage assignment orders, notices of payroll deduction, and tax levies have priority over other types of garnishment, your first impulse may be to answer that no funds will be withheld because a prior garnishment is in effect which has priority over the new garnishment. Ordinarily, this is the correct answer. But in some cases, it is incorrect.

Even though a wage assignment is in effect, there may still be non-exempt earnings available for withholding under the writ, but only if the amount being withheld under the wage assignment is less than 25% of the employee's net earnings (or 60% in the case of a child support garnishment).

For garnishments other than child support, the maximum amount that can be withheld is 25% of an employee's net earnings. And for most garnishments, if a prior garnishment is in effect, the second garnishment is not effective until the prior garnishment ends.

But wage assignment orders and notices of payroll deduction are not exactly garnishments; they are court and administrative orders. And they do not end in sixty days; they go on until the support obligation ends, sometimes for years.

The general rule is: If the OSE or IRS levy is taking 25% or more of your employee's net earnings, you would not withhold under a new garnishment because all of your employee's non-exempt earnings are being withheld under a prior levy. But if the wage assignment order is taking less than 25% of your employee's net earnings, you would withhold the difference under the non-priority writ of garnishment.

The test is simply: Is the order taking more or less than 25% of your employee's net earnings? If less than 25%, then under the new garnishment you would withhold the difference between the order and 25% of your employee's net earnings. (In the case of a child support garnishment, use 60% in the above calculations.)

Assume in Rick's case, where he is earning $2,500 per pay period, with $500 withheld for taxes, that you are withholding $1,000 per pay period under an OSE withholding order. Since $1,000 is 50% of Rick's net pay of $2,000, there is nothing left to withhold under the new garnishment (unless it is a garnishment for child support for 60% in which case the additional 10% or $200 can be withheld for the child support garnishment).

Now assume only $250 is being withheld from Rick's wages under the OSE withholding order. That is only 12.5% of Rick's net earnings, so you would withhold the difference under the new garnishment, which would be $250 per pay period.

A judgment creditor's attorney may tell you that all of this is incorrect, and that the "correct" way to calculate the withholding under the new garnishment would be to treat the wage assignment order as a "mandatory deduction" from Rick's net wages, then take 25% of whatever is left over. It sounds good for the creditor, and is easier to calculate, but it is certainly not right, as is demonstrated below.

Again, assume Rick earns $2,500 gross, less $500 tax withholding, leaving $2,000 net earnings per pay period. Assume OSE is getting 50% of Rick's net earnings per pay period, or $1,000. If that $1,000 is treated as a mandatory deduction, Rick's net earnings are reduced to $1,000 per pay period. Then, if you took another 25% under the new garnishment, Rick would receive only $750 net earnings per pay period, after a total of 62.5% of his earnings were withheld under the OSE levy and the new garnishment. This is not only wrong, it is illegal!

This scenario would be even worse if the new garnishment was for child support. Imagine: After $1,000 is deducted for OSE, another 60% of the remaining $1,000 would be taken for the child support garnishment, leaving Rick with only $400 per pay period. This isn't right, no matter what anybody tells you.

The current state garnishment answer form provides for deduction of any OSE or IRS levy amounts from the employee's non-exempt earnings. By subtracting the amount of the levy from the non-exempt earnings, you determine the amount to be withheld under the writ of garnishment. If the levy amount is greater than the non-exempt earnings, then you withhold $0.00.

Obviously, figuring out how much to withhold under competing, conflicting garnishments and wage assignments can present challenges. If you have any questions about how to withhold under a new garnishment when you already have a wage assignment order or notice of payroll deduction in effect, call your attorney.

F. EXEMPTION CLAIMS

At the same time you are served with a Writ of Garnishment, a copy is mailed to your employee, along with an Exemption Claim form. If your employee claims an exemption, he or she may have the amount of withholding reduced.

For example, if the garnishment is for child support, your employee, Rick, may claim that, because he is supporting another family or child, he is entitled to a greater exemption (50% instead of 40%). Rick would have to fill out and sign the Exemption Claim form and file it with the court; you would probably get a copy. At this point, you would continue withholding. If the garnishing creditor agrees, you would be instructed to give Rick the larger exemption, and you would reduce your withholding. If the garnishing creditor disagrees, there would be a court hearing to decide whether Rick is entitled to the exemption he claimed. You would then receive a court order either directing you to give Rick a larger exemption, or stating that you should continue withholding at the same rate.

In the case of an exemption claim, or in any case, you should not alter your withholding except upon written instruction from the garnishing creditor, or upon receipt of a court order. Never do what your employee tells you to do without something to back it up. Some employers who believed their employees when they said they had "taken care of it" have paid a price for their gullibility.

G. INSUFFICIENT EARNINGS

State and federal employment laws have fixed minimum amounts which must be paid to employees regardless of garnishments and wage levies. These amounts must be stated in a "continuing lien" garnishment. They are the greater of either:

(1) Thirty times the federal minimum hourly wage at the time the earnings are payable; or

(2) Seventy-five percent of the disposable earnings of the defendant.

Item (2) has already been discussed; this is the 25% cap on withholding (which increases to 60% if the garnishment is for child support). But how do you calculate thirty times the minimum hourly wage?

Actually, you don't need to calculate it; the federal minimum amounts must be stated in the answer form. [See Appendix 4; RCW 6.27.340.] If those amounts are not provided, or the amounts provided are incorrect, the you may treat the writ as one that is not a continuing lien and withhold only what you owe the employee at the moment the writ was served.

The federal minimum amounts usually come into play with part-time employees, or unskilled laborers earning at or near minimum wage. (Actually, the federal-minimum rule provides an unintended shelter for part-timers, who can render their earnings garnishment-proof by holding only part-time jobs, thus never earning more than the federal minimum at any one job.)

The basic rule is: You must pay your employee the federal minimum amount or 75% of his net earnings (or 60% if the garnishment is for child support), whichever is greater. If you don't, you are breaking the law.

The only time this usually becomes a problem is when you are withholding under a wage assignment order, OSE notice of payroll deduction, or IRS notice of levy. Each of these orders may direct you to withhold up to 50% of your employee's net earnings, which could leave your employee with less than the federal minimum amount of net pay. Also, if another garnishment is served, it can really complicate things. In such cases, ask your attorney for advice before proceeding.

H. TIP INCOME

Restaurant owners face a common problem when it comes to garnishments directed to their waiters and waitresses: how to account for cash tips?

In some restaurants, this problem is solved by "pooling" tips and distributing them on an equal basis to all employees on a given shift; the employer can simply deduct 25% of the garnished employee's share of the tips and hold it under the writ. Or the employer can hold tips paid by credit or debit card until the next pay period and withhold from tip income at that time.

Because the employer has control of tips paid by debit or credit card, the employer must account for those tips when answering and withholding under a writ of garnishment.

In most cases, there is really nothing the employer can do about cash tips, since the employer technically does not "owe" the tips to the employer—they are gratuitous "gifts" from customers. So unless the employee is willing to voluntarily account for tips and withhold from them him or herself, or unless the employer "pools" tips and distributes them to employees, an employer is powerless.

If tip income cannot be reached by an employer for withholding, the employer may only withhold from the hourly wages or regular salary of the restaurant employee.

But what if the restaurant has reduced the tip-earning employee's hourly wages? This practice is permitted by federal law for food-service employees who earn tips. Thus, arguably, the employer would have created an artificial shelter for his or her employee, who may, by virtue of the reduced hourly wage, earn less than the federal minimum amount, while still reaping tip income well in excess of the federal minimum.

There are no known court decisions on this issue, but it seems reasonable that, in order to properly withhold under a garnishment directed to a waiter or waitress, the employer should require the employee to account for his or her tip income during the sixty-day effective period of the writ. Of course, the employee will be reluctant to do so, and will likely under-report his or her tip income. But you probably can't control that unless you follow the employee around from table to table counting his or her tip income every night for two months—hardly a reasonable thing for a busy restaurant manager to be doing. In these cases, do your best.

I. FAILURE TO ANSWER THE WRIT

As mentioned previously, if you fail to answer a Writ of Garnishment within twenty days from the date of service, you may be in for an expensive lesson.

What will probably happen if you fail to answer the writ and don't respond to the ten-day notice of default is that a zealous creditor's attorney will obtain a judgment against you for the amount due from your employee. Fortunately, a notice is required before the default judgment can be entered against you, but a surprisingly large number of employers still don't respond.

When you receive the ten-day default notice, you need to file and serve the answer immediately. That is the only notice you are going to get.

If you fail to answer in response to the default notice and a judgment is entered, then at the moment you find out about the default judgment, or at the moment you find out your bank account or other asset has been garnished, YOU MUST ACT IMMEDIATELY!

You have only SEVEN DAYS! to file a motion to set aside the default judgment. Your right to have the default judgment set aside is automatic and absolute, but only if you act promptly.

CONTACT YOUR ATTORNEY IMMEDIATELY IF A DEFAULT JUDGMENT IS ENTERED AGAINST YOU BASED ON YOUR FAILURE TO ANSWER A WRIT OF GARNISHMENT!

In most cases, if you act promptly, the default judgment can be set aside as a matter of right, but even so, you will end up paying one or more of the following:

- Your own attorney's fees and costs;

- The judgment creditor's attorney's fees and costs; and

- The amount you should have withheld from the employee, or $100, whichever is less.

If you do not file your motion within seven days, you may end up stuck paying the entire judgment owed by the debtor—whether or not he or she was ever an employee of your business!

In some cases where you end up with a default judgment for failing to answer a Writ of Garnishment, there may be a cheaper, easier option than moving to have the default judgment set aside. If the judgment amount owed by your employee is relatively small, you may prefer to simply buy the judgment for the remaining balance due. Once you own the judgment, you can either garnish your own employee's wages, or (with your employee's permission) deduct a percentage of his or her wages each pay period until the judgment is paid off.

In cases where a default judgment has been entered against you for failing to timely answer a garnishment, taking assignment of a judgment may make good economic sense. Although you must initially pay for the judgment, you have recourse against your employee and in most cases will get that money back over time.

If you choose instead to challenge the default judgment, or the validity of the garnishment, you will incur several hundred or thousand dollars of your own attorney's fees, and if you lose, you will also have to pay the judgment creditor's attorney's fees.

Discuss this option with your attorney before proceeding, to make sure you do it correctly.

J.   ANSWERING IMPROPERLY

Again, if your answer is improper, for any reason, you may also end up paying somebody's attorney's fees—or everybody's.

There are various ways to improperly answer a Writ of Garnishment. The most common are:

- Failing to sign the answer;

- Leaving blank spaces that are required to be filled in;

- Not filling in correct dollar amounts;

- Addition and multiplication errors;

- Insufficient withholding; and

- Overwithholding.

According to Washington's garnishment statute, YOU MUST SIGN THE ANSWER! DO NOT answer on a Post-It Note; DO NOT scribble an unsigned answer on the front of the Writ; DO

NOT make a phone call; DO NOT send the paperwork back unsigned. Fill out the answer form, and SIGN IT! An unsigned answer is deemed no answer, and has the same effect as not answering.

To avoid any problems, fill out the answer completely; try to leave no blank spaces. Write "-0-", "N/A", or "None" if appropriate; in all other spaces, provide the requested information, and make a simple but detailed accounting of your employee's wages. Then sign it and mail it back.

Another common problem is not filling in the correct dollar amounts. A judgment creditor's attorney probably won't know the difference, but if you purposely underreport your employee's wages and the creditor's attorney catches you, you can expect to end up in court and paying somebody's attorney's fees, as well as your own. In addition, whoever signed the answer form can face perjury or fraud charges if he or she knew that the wages were being purposely under-reported.

Addition and multiplication errors are another common problem, which leads to insufficient withholding or overwithholding. Check and recheck your figures carefully, to make sure you are withholding no more or no less than required by the writ.

If you find your answer to the garnishment is incorrect, you may amend your answer to reflect the correct amount of wages or withholding, and you may adjust your withholding accordingly. Mail a copy of your amended answer to the court, the judgment creditor, and to your employee. Remember to sign each copy of the amended answer. If you don't have a blank answer form left over, simply write and sign a letter containing the corrected figures, and mail that to the court, the judgment creditor, and your attorney. Or you may prefer to create a custom answer form for your company's use. Large corporations such as Boeing use customized letters as answer forms.

K. CONTROVERSION OF ANSWER

If the judgment creditor does not believe your answer, for any reason, he or she may "controvert" your answer by filing an affidavit stating in particular why he or she believes your answer is wrong. RCW 6.27.210.

This controverting affidavit must be filed within twenty days of the filing of your answer and served on you and the employee. If no controverting affidavit is filed, then even if your answer is wrong, the judgment creditor can do nothing about it after twenty days.

Controversion often occurs when an employer lies in its answer to the Writ of Garnishment, by claiming the employee does not work there, or that the employee is not earning enough money for withholding, or when the employee backdates payments to the employee to make it appear the debt had already been discharged. If the judgment creditor knows the answer is wrong, and can prove it, he or she will not hesitate to controvert the answer. Another common cause for controversion is failure to withhold from year-end bonuses or other periodic payments paid in addition to regular wages. Or, if you made a math error, and refuse to correct it when it is brought to your attention, a controverting affidavit might be filed to coerce you into correcting your answer.

If a controverting affidavit is filed, it must be served on you by mail or personal service. Once received, you should review it carefully and decide whether or not the judgment creditor is correct. If the judgment creditor is correct, you should amend your answer so it conforms with the statements made in the controverting affidavit.

If you believe your answer is correct, and disagree with the controverting affidavit, you should contact your attorney before proceeding.

If you dispute the controverting affidavit, you have twenty days to file your own affidavit stating why you believe your answer is correct, and why the controverting affidavit is wrong. Your attorney should help you prepare this affidavit, as it will be the only evidence you can present in the event the dispute goes to trial. Furthermore, only an attorney can represent a corporation or LLC in court proceedings.

After that twenty days has passed, whether or not you have filed a response to the controverting affidavit, either you or the judgment creditor may note a court hearing to determine whether a trial is necessary regarding the issue of whether or not your answer is correct. Again, your attorney should be involved in this hearing. If your business is a corporation or LLC, it must be represented by an attorney at the controversion hearing.

At the hearing, the court will consider the controverting affidavit and your responsive affidavit, and listen to the arguments of your attorney and the judgment creditor's attorney. Depending upon how it goes, the judge could decide that your answer is correct, in which case you are entitled to an award of attorney's fees and costs for your trouble. Or the judge may decide your answer is wrong, in which case you might have to pay the judgment creditor's attorney's fees and costs. Or the judge may decide the issue is too complex to be decided solely on the affidavits, and order a trial on the issue. Although this would probably be a short trial, it would not be cheap, and the loser would be required to pay the winner's attorney's fees and costs. For this reason, you should answer honestly when answering a Writ of Garnishment, and you should double check your answer to make sure it is accurate before you sign it.

L.   WITHHOLDING IMPROPERLY

As mentioned previously, accounting errors may result in over-withholding and underwithholding, which can wind you up in court paying attorney's fees. Again, check and recheck your calculations before signing the answer. Under-withholding in your employee's favor may result in a challenge by the judgment creditor; over-withholding in the judgment creditor's favor may result in a challenge by your employee. Either could result in an expensive, time-consuming court hearing.

M.   EMPLOYEE QUITS OR IS FIRED

What if your employee quits after the garnishment is served? This happens quite often, and you should know what to do if it does happen.

Suppose a garnishment is served on April 1st, at which time Rick is earning $2,500 gross earnings per semi-monthly pay period. Rick quits that day, when he gets notice of the garnishment.

If Rick is an hourly employee with no severance or accrued vacation pay coming, you probably would not have any earnings to withhold at the next pay period. You would answer that Rick quit on April 1st and that you owed him $0.00 wages, or that his small paycheck for one day's work did not net earnings over the federal minimum and $0.00 was withheld.

If at the time Rick quits, you owe him accrued vacation or sick pay or any bonus or severance pay, 25% of that pay must be withheld. Vacation and severance pay are types of "earnings" under Washington's garnishment statute.

CONSPIRACY AND FRAUD

In some cases, an employee "quits" when a garnishment is served, then is "re-hired" after the employer has answered the writ by stating "the employee no longer works here." Typically, the employer approves of and aids in this ruse. You should not allow yourself to become a part of this fraud. It could result not only in civil penalties, but you could be charged with a crime, such as criminal conspiracy, fraud, perjury, or contempt of court.

Even if the judgment creditor does not find out about this charade during the sixty-day effective period of the writ, it may assert a claim against you for fraud or misrepresentation if it finds out later on. If you unwittingly participate in this fraud, that is excusable, but if you take any knowing part in lying or cheating in the garnishment process, you can be held liable, not only for civil sanctions but possibly also for criminal penalties. This is true in every case where you lie or cheat on your answer form or in your withholding practices. Accordingly, you should never take part in any of these common deceptions:

> "Firing" your employee, then "re-hiring" the employee after answering that the employee was fired, to avoid withholding earnings.

> Paying wages under the table so you don't have to report them in the answer form (this might also be considered tax evasion).

> Agreeing not to pay your employee, who keeps working, until after the sixty-day effective period of the writ has elapsed.

> Laying off your employee so he or she can draw unemployment benefits while the garnishment is pending, then re-hiring your employee as soon as the writ is no longer effective.

> Giving your employee a pre-dated "advance" paycheck so you don't have to withhold under the garnishment.

These examples are plainly and simply fraud, which will be punished if discovered. Protect yourself! Don't get involved in schemes designed to cheat the garnishment process.

EMPLOYEE IS REHIRED

If an employee really quits and is subsequently rehired, the garnishment may still be effective against any earnings you pay the employee during the sixty-day effective period of the writ.

Assume Rick quits on April 1st, and you answer that Rick quit and you are not withholding any wages. Then Rick reapplies on April 16th, and you rehire him and continue paying him wages on regular pay periods thereafter. Since the garnishment is effective for sixty days, you must continue withholding after Rick's re-hire. If you fail to withhold Rick's earnings during the following pay periods up through May 31st, you could be liable to the judgment creditor for those amounts you should have withheld.

If you re-hire a terminated employee during the sixty days following service of a Writ of Garnishment, you should amend your answer and continue withholding.

A loophole exists in the garnishment statute by which a garnished employee could conceivably quit, then be rehired after twenty days, and avoid having his or her wages garnished, but if you allow this practice, it makes you look bad, or worse, unless you promptly disclose the employee's re-hire to the garnishing creditor.

N. WAGE ASSIGNMENTS

Another type of wage withholding occurs under a "wage assignment," which is a voluntary agreement by your employee to allow a certain amount of his or her wages to be paid to a judgment creditor. (Not the same as a wage assignment for withholding of child support, which is court ordered.)

Typically this arrangement is made after the judgment creditor has garnished once or twice, and the employee realizes the judgment creditor is not going to go away. Also, since up to $400 attorney's fees and costs are charged to the employee each time a garnishment is issued, it will save the employee hundreds, even thousands of dollars, to agree to a voluntary wage assignment.

The wage assignment can take many forms, usually depending upon the employer's requirements. Some employers require a court order; others require a formal, notarized assignment; others require only a letter signed by their employee; others require only verbal directions from their employee; some employers refuse to allow assignment of wages except by court order.

If you do permit this type of assignment of wages, you should insist upon a letter signed by your employee, preferably signed in your presence or notarized so you can be sure your employee signed the letter.

Under a wage assignment, the federal minimum amounts still apply, so in all cases, you should still pay your employee the federal minimum amount, or 75% of his or her net wages if the federal minimum is exceeded. You should comply with the federal minimum requirement, and require that any wage assignment you accept contain language to that effect.

In cases where your employee requests that you withhold a larger amount, you can refuse to do so. You do not have to comply with a wage assignment, except a mandatory wage assignment for child support, or a court-ordered wage assignment. And you should never agree to entry of a court-ordered wage assignment under any circumstances.

A major downside to wage assignments is usually overlooked by employees and sometimes even by judgment creditors: If a garnishment from another creditor is served while a wage assignment is pending, the wage assignment does not have priority over the garnishment because it is not a "mandatory" deduction nor a prior garnishment. So, if you are withholding under a voluntary wage assignment when a garnishment is served, you and your employee have a problem.

Depending upon the language of the wage assignment, you could do three things: (1) stop withholding under the wage assignment and start withholding under the Writ of Garnishment instead; (2) continue withholding under the wage assignment and answer the writ by saying you are withholding under a previous garnishment; or (3) withhold under both the wage assignment and garnishment.

The best option is (1)—stop withholding under the wage assignment and start withholding under the garnishment. Then, when the writ is satisfied, you can resume withholding under the wage assignment—unless another garnishment is served.

Option (2) will get you into trouble if the judgment creditor challenges your answer.

Option (3) may be a violation of state or federal laws, particularly if you withhold more than the employee's exempt amounts or minimum federal amounts.

As noted above, if the wage assignment is in the form of a court order, you must comply with it or face contempt charges. Court-ordered wage assignments technically are supposed to be issued only for child support, but judges sometimes sign them in other cases when everyone is in agreement. Unfortunately, this can get you into trouble. But a court order is a court order. But what happens is that, if you are served with a garnishment while a wage assignment is pending, you will be faced with two conflicting court orders, one telling you to withhold under the wage assignment, the other telling you to withhold under the Writ of Garnishment. You cannot possibly do both, so what do you do?

In such cases, you should first call your attorney and alert him or her to the situation. Then notify the court, your employee, and both judgment creditors of the situation, in writing. Then withhold under both the wage assignment and the garnishment, and continue holding the funds until you receive instructions, in the form of a court order, telling you what to do.

What should happen is the garnishing creditor will note a hearing and the court should enter an order ruling that the garnishment has priority over the wage assignment. You should not try to guess what to do; if you guess wrong, you may end up owing more than either creditor is trying to collect.

Unfortunately, many employees who enter into wage assignment agreements don't realize that voluntary wage assignments don't have priority over other garnishments. So, what often happens is that employers, when served with a garnishment, will withhold under the garnishment, and also continue to withhold from the wage assignment. Since the employee authorized this, the employer may have every right to do it.

A well-drafted wage assignment can anticipate and resolve many issues before they arise, but the employer usually isn't in a position to want or need to pay an attorney to draft such a document. It may be better to simply not accept voluntary wage assignment agreements and avoid potential problems.

O.   EMPLOYEE FILES BANKRUPTCY

Another problem which may arise during the garnishment process is what to do when your employee files bankruptcy. Faced with mounting pressure by creditors, bankruptcy may be your employee's only option. Unfortunately, this can create complications for the unwary employer.

Pursuant to Section 362 of the Bankruptcy Code, all actions against the bankrupt debtor's assets are stayed pending the conclusion of the bankruptcy case. This includes garnishments by judgment creditors.

Usually when an employee files bankruptcy, the employee and his or her attorney will insist that you immediately stop withholding wages, citing Section 362 of the Bankruptcy Code, and also insisting that you release any withheld earnings to the employee.

However, you may think you should not stop withholding until you receive a court order directing you to stop withholding. The filing if a bankruptcy petition constitutes an order for relief, which includes the automatic stay provisions of Section 362. The bankruptcy order for relief requires that you stop withholding. Get a copy of the order for relief before you stop withholding, to be sure that the employee really has filed bankruptcy.

The stay imposed by Section 362 generally applies to actions by creditors. Because of the stay, the judgment creditor is required to cease collection efforts, and to quash the garnishment. It is a good idea to contact the creditor's attorney and ask for a letter affirming that the bankruptcy stay is in effect and directing that you stop withholding.

Also, until you receive a court order directing you to release the earnings already withheld, you should not release those earnings to anyone. Your employee may be entitled to claim those withheld earnings as exempt property, but if he or she does not claim the withheld earnings as exempt, the judgment creditor may still have a valid lien against those earnings. The bankruptcy trustee may also have a claim against those withheld earnings. Hold onto them until a court order or the bankruptcy trustee directs their release.

If you release those earnings to the employee as soon as your employee files bankruptcy, you may end up liable to the judgment creditor for interfering with its lien rights. If you release those funds to the judgment creditor, you may suffer the wrath of the bankruptcy court for willful violation of the automatic stay.

Finally, you can't fire your employee just because he or she files bankruptcy. Federal law prohibits private employers from discriminating against employees who have filed bankruptcy. The only exceptions may be for employees whose licensing, bonding, or security clearance is affected by their bankruptcy filing. If by filing bankruptcy they are no longer qualified for the position (because, for example, a bankruptcy filing cancels their bond), that is a non-discriminatory ground for termination. Likewise, if employment is at-will, the employee could be terminated for other reasons, which should be well documented.

APPENDIX

The Appendix includes the following sample forms and resources to be used as reference for identifying, completing, and processing garnishment paperwork.

1   Worksheet for Withholding

2   Sample Writ of Garnishment

3   Sample Writ for Continuing Lien

4   Sample First Answer Form

5   Attachment to Answer Form

6   Sample Judgment on Answer and Order to Pay

7   Excerpts from Washington's Garnishment Statute--RCW 6.27

APPENDIX 1

GARNISHMENT WITHHOLDING WORKSHEET

Employee: _____

Date Writ Served: _____ Answer Due: _____

Documents Served: ☐ Writ   ☐ Continuing Lien on Earnings*

                       ☐ First Answer Form

                       ☐ Other (list all other documents received)

_____

Date Answer Prepared/Mailed: _____

Creditor/Attorney: _____

_____

Court/Address: _____

_____

Pay Period: _____

Employee's Gross Earnings: $_____

Less Mandatory Deductions: $_____

Employee's Net Earnings: $_____

(Is above amount less than minimum amounts per pay period listed in Answer form? If so, do not withhold. Answer still required.)

Employee's Net Earnings: $_____

Less 75% Exempt Amount: $_____

(Different percentage is exempt for child support garnishments; refer to Writ for applicable percentage if garnishment is for child support.)

Less Liens/Child Support: $_____

Amount to Withhold: $_____

*Withholding under continuing lien on earnings continues for each pay period sixty days after the date of service of the Writ. Complete a separate worksheet for each applicable pay period.

Are you holding any funds or property belonging to Employee other than earnings? If so, list below and in your answer form and withhold those funds/property items from employee pending court order.

_____

_____

*Withholding funds property until you receive a court order directing you to pay/deliver to the court or creditor's attorney.

Date Order to Pay Received: _____

Date Funds/Property Delivered: _____

Notes: _____

_____

_____

APPENDIX 2

WRIT OF GARNISHMENT (NOT CONTINUING LIEN)

SUPERIOR COURT OF WASHINGTON
COUNTY OF KING

FRIENDLY FINANCE COMPANY,

                            Plaintiff,

vs.

RICK SMITH,

                         Defendant(s).

YOUR COMPANY,

                      Garnishee.

NO. 11-2-12345-6 XYZ

WRIT OF GARNISHMENT (DEBTS OTHER THAN EARNINGS--AFTER JUDGMENT)
(WRG or $WRG)
☐ This garnishment is based on a judgment or order for child support.

The State of Washington to: YOUR COMPANY, Garnishee; and
To: RICK SMITH, Defendant(s).

The plaintiff in this action has applied for a Writ of Garnishment against you, claiming that the above-named defendant is indebted to plaintiff and that the amount to be held to satisfy the indebtedness is $5,530.00, consisting of:

Balance of Judgment:		$5,000.00
Interest under Judgment from 4/1/2018 to 6/1/2018:		$100.00
Taxable Costs and Attorneys' Fees:		$430.00
Estimated Garnishment Costs:		
Filing and Ex Parte Fees:	$35.00	
Service and Affidavit Fees:	$65.00	
Postage and Costs of Certified Mail:	$10.00	
Answer Fee or Fees:	$20.00	
Garnishment Attorney Fees:	$300.00	
Other:	$_____	
Total estimated garnishment costs:		$430.00
TOTAL:		$_____
Plus Per Day Rate of Estimated Interest:		$ 1.64 Per day

WRIT OF GARNISHMENT - 1 OF 2

YOU ARE COMMANDED, unless otherwise directed by the court, by the attorney of record for the plaintiff, or by this writ, not to pay any debt, other than earnings, owed to the defendant at the time this writ was served and not to deliver, sell, or transfer, or recognize any sale or transfer of, any personal property or effects of the defendant in your possession or control at the time when this writ was served. Any such payment delivery, sale, or transfer is void to the extent necessary to satisfy the plaintiff's claim and costs for this writ with interest.

YOU ARE ALSO COMMANDED to answer this writ according to the instructions in this writ and in the answer forms and, within 20 days after the service of the writ upon you, to mail or deliver the original of such answer to the court, one copy to the plaintiff or the plaintiff's attorney, and one copy to the defendant, at the addresses listed at the bottom of this writ.

If you owe the defendant a debt payable in money in excess of the amount set forth in the first paragraph of this writ, hold only the amount set forth in the first paragraph and any processing fee if one is charged and release all additional funds or property to defendant.

IF YOU FAIL TO ANSWER THIS WRIT AS COMMANDED, A JUDGMENT MAY BE ENTERED AGAINST YOU FOR THE FULL AMOUNT OF THE PLAINTIFF'S CLAIM AGAINST THE DEFENDANT WITH ACCRUING INTEREST, ATTORNEY FEES, AND COSTS WHETHER OR NOT YOU OWE ANYTHING TO THE DEFENDANT. IF YOU PROPERLY ANSWER THIS WRIT, ANY JUDGMENT AGAINST YOU WILL NOT EXCEED THE AMOUNT OF ANY NONEXEMPT DEBT OR THE VALUE OF ANY NONEXEMPT PROPERTY OR EFFECTS IN YOUR POSSESSION OR CONTROL.

JUDGMENT MAY ALSO BE ENTERED AGAINST THE DEFENDANT FOR COSTS AND FEES INCURRED BY THE PLAINTIFF.

☐ Witness, the Honorable /S/ JUDGE McJUDGE, Judge of the above-entitled Court, and the seal thereof, on June 1, 2018.

/s/ Attorney Name	/s/ Clerk of Court
AttorneyName	Clerk of the Court
701 Pike Street, Suite 1700, Seattle WA 98101	By:/s/ Deputy Clerk
Address	
RICK SMITH	516 Third Avenue, Seattle, WA 98104
Name of Defendant	Address
1313 Mockingbird Lane, Seattle, WA 98013	
Address of Defendant	

WRIT OF GARNISHMENT - 2 OF 2

APPENDIX 3

WRIT OF GARNISHMENT
(CONTINUING LIEN ON EARNINGS)

SUPERIOR COURT OF WASHINGTON
COUNTY OF KING

FRIENDLY FINANCE COMPANY,	NO. 11-2-12345-6 XYZ
Plaintiff.	WRIT OF GARNISHMENT
vs.	(CONTINUING LIEN ON EARNINGS--AFTER JUDGMENT)
RICK SMITH,	(WRG or $WRG)
Defendant(s).	☐ This garnishment is based on a judgment or order for child support.
YOUR COMPANY,	
Garnishee.	

The State of Washington to: YOUR COMPANY, Garnishee; and
To: RICK SMITH, Defendant(s).

The plaintiff in this action has applied for a Writ of Garnishment against you, claiming that the above-named defendant is indebted to plaintiff and that the amount to be held to satisfy the indebtedness is $5,530.00, consisting of:

Balance of Judgment:		$5,000.00
Interest under Judgment from 4/1/2018 to 6/1/2018:		$100.00
Taxable Costs and Attorneys' Fees:		$430.00
Estimated Garnishment Costs:		
Filing and Ex Parte Fees:	$35.00	
Service and Affidavit Fees:	$65.00	
Postage and Costs of Certified Mail:	$10.00	
Answer Fee or Fees:	$20.00	
Garnishment Attorney Fees:	$300.00	
Other:	$_____	
Total estimated garnishment costs:		$430.00
TOTAL		$_____
Plus Per Day Rate of Estimated Interest:		$ 1.64 Per day

WRIT OF GARNISHMENT - 1 OF 3

THIS IS A WRIT FOR A CONTINUING LIEN. THE GARNISHEE SHALL HOLD the nonexempt portion of the defendant's earnings due at the time of service of this writ and shall also hold the defendant's nonexempt earnings that accrue through the last payroll period ending on or before SIXTY days after the date of service of this writ. HOWEVER, IF THE GARNISHEE IS PRESENTLY HOLDING THE NONEXEMPT PORTION OF THE DEFENDANT'S EARNINGS UNDER A PREVIOUSLY SERVED WRIT FOR A CONTINUING LIEN, THE GARNISHEE SHALL HOLD UNDER THIS WRIT only the defendant's nonexempt earnings that accrue from the date the previously served writ or writs terminate and through the last payroll period ending on or before sixty days after the date of termination of the previous writ or writs. IN EITHER CASE, THE GARNISHEE SHALL STOP WITHHOLDING WHEN THE SUM WITHHELD EQUALS THE AMOUNT STATED IN THIS WRIT OF GARNISHMENT.

YOU ARE HEREBY COMMANDED, unless otherwise directed by the court, by the attorney of record for the plaintiff, or by this writ, not to pay any debt, whether earnings subject to this garnishment or any other debt, owed to the defendant at the time this writ was served and not to deliver, sell, or transfer, or recognize any sale or transfer of, any personal property or effects of the defendant in your possession or control at the time when this writ was served. Any such payment, delivery, sale, or transfer is void to the extent necessary to satisfy the plaintiff's claim and costs for this writ with interest.

YOU ARE FURTHER COMMANDED to answer this writ according to the instructions in this writ and in the answer forms and, within twenty days after the service of the writ upon you, to mail or deliver the original of such answer to the court, one copy to the plaintiff or the plaintiff's attorney, and one copy to the defendant, at the addresses listed at the bottom of this writ.

If, at the time this writ was served, you owed the defendant any earnings (that is, wages, salary, commission, bonus, tips, or other compensation for personal services or any periodic payments pursuant to a nongovernmental pension or retirement program), the defendant is entitled to receive amounts that are exempt from garnishment under federal and state law. You must pay the exempt amounts to the defendant on the day you would customarily pay the compensation or other periodic payment. As more fully explained in the answer, the basic exempt amount is the greater of seventy-five percent of disposable earnings or a minimum amount determined by reference to the employee's pay period, to be calculated as provided in the answer. However, if this writ carries a statement in the heading that "This garnishment is based on a judgment or order for child support," the basic exempt amount is fifty percent of disposable earnings.

YOU MAY DEDUCT A PROCESSING FEE FROM THE REMAINDER OF THE EMPLOYEE'S EARNINGS AFTER WITHHOLDING UNDER THIS WRIT. THE PROCESSING FEE MAY NOT EXCEED TWENTY DOLLARS FOR THE FIRST ANSWER AND TEN DOLLARS AT THE TIME YOU SUBMIT THE SECOND ANSWER.

If you owe the defendant a debt payable in money in excess of the amount set forth in the first paragraph of this writ, hold only the amount set forth in the first paragraph and any processing fee if one is charged and release all additional funds or property to defendant.

WRIT OF GARNISHMENT - 2 OF 3

IF YOU FAIL TO ANSWER THIS WRIT AS COMMANDED, A JUDGMENT MAY BE ENTERED AGAINST YOU FOR THE FULL AMOUNT OF THE PLAINTIFF'S CLAIM AGAINST THE DEFENDANT WITH ACCRUING INTEREST, ATTORNEY FEES, AND COSTS WHETHER OR NOT YOU OWE ANYTHING TO THE DEFENDANT. IF YOU PROPERLY ANSWER THIS WRIT, ANY JUDGMENT AGAINST YOU WILL NOT EXCEED THE AMOUNT OF ANY NONEXEMPT DEBT OR THE VALUE OF ANY NONEXEMPT PROPERTY OR EFFECTS IN YOUR POSSESSION OR CONTROL.

JUDGMENT MAY ALSO BE ENTERED AGAINST THE DEFENDANT FOR COSTS AND FEES INCURRED BY THE PLAINTIFF.

☐ Witness, the Honorable /S/ JUDGE McJUDGE, Judge of the above-entitled Court, and the seal thereof, on June 1, 2018.

/s/ Attorney Name	/s/ Clerk of Court
AttorneyName	Clerk of the Court
701 Pike Street, Suite 1700, Seattle WA 98101	By:/s/ Deputy Clerk
Address	
RICK SMITH	516 Third Avenue, Seattle, WA 98104
Name of Defendant	Address
1313 Mockingbird Lane, Seattle, WA 98013	
Address of Defendant	

WRIT OF GARNISHMENT - 3 OF 3

APPENDIX 4

SAMPLE FIRST ANSWER TO WRIT OF GARNISHMENT
(CONTINUING LIEN)

SUPERIOR COURT OF WASHINGTON
COUNTY OF KING

NO. 11-2-12345-6 XYZ

FRIENDLY FINANCE COMPANY,

                     Plaintiff,

vs.

RICK SMITH,

                     Defendant(s),

YOUR COMPANY,

                     Garnishee.

FIRST ANSWER TO WRIT OF GARNISHMENT FOR CONTINUING LIEN ON EARNINGS (ANWRGR)

SECTION I: If you are withholding the defendant's nonexempt earnings under a previously served writ for a continuing lien, answer only sections I and III of this form and mail or deliver the forms as directed in the writ. Withhold from the defendant's future nonexempt earnings as directed in the writ, and a second set of answer forms will be forwarded to you later.

If you are NOT withholding the defendant's earnings under a previously served writ for a continuing lien, answer this ENTIRE form and mail or deliver the forms as directed in the writ. A second set of answer forms will be forwarded to you later for subsequently withheld earnings.

ANSWER: I am presently holding the defendant's nonexempt earnings under a previous writ served on _____ (date) that will terminate not later than _____ (date). **[IF YOU ARE WITHHOLDING UNDER A PRIOR WRIT, FILL IN DATES]**

On the date the Writ of Garnishment was issued as indicated by the date appearing on the last page of the writ, **[CHECK THE APPROPRIATE BOXES/FILL IN APPROPRIATE BLANKS]**

(A) The defendant: (check one) ☒ was ☐ was not employed by garnishee. If not employed and you have no possession or control of any funds of defendant, indicate the last day of employment:_____; and complete section III of this answer and mail or deliver the forms as directed in the writ;

(B) The defendant: (check one) ☐ did ☒ did not maintain a financial account with garnishee; and

(C) The garnishee: (check one) ☒ did ☐ did not have possession of or control over any funds, personal property, or effects of the defendant. (List all of defendant's personal property or effects in your possession or control on the bottom of the last page of this answer form or attach a schedule if necessary.)

SECTION II: At the time of service of the Writ of Garnishment on the garnishee, there was due and owing from the garnishee to the above-named defendant $ 1,250.00

1ˢᵗ ANS TO WRIT OF GARN FOR CONT LIEN ON EARNINGS (ANWRGR) - Page 1 of 3
WPF GARN 01.0750 (06/2012) - RCW 6.27.340

This writ attaches a maximum of _____ % (percent) of the Defendant's disposable earnings (that is, compensation payable for personal services, whether called wages, salary, commission, bonus, or otherwise, and including periodic payments pursuant to a nongovernmental pension or retirement program). Calculate the attachable amount as follows:

Gross Earnings: [AMOUNTS ARE EXAMPLE ONLY] $ 1,250.00 (1)

Less deductions required by law (Social Security, federal withholding tax, etc. Do not include deductions for child support orders or Government liens here. Deduct child support orders and liens on line 7): $ 250.00 (2)

Disposable Earnings (subtract line 2 from line 1): $ 1,000.00 (3)

Enter 75 % (percent) of line 3 $ 750.00 (4)

Enter one of the following exempt amounts*: $ _____ (5)
If paid Weekly $_____   Semi-monthly $_____
       Bi-weekly $_____   Monthly $_____
[THESE AMOUNTS SHOULD BE FILLED IN ON THE ANSWER FORM YOU RECEIVE]
*These are minimum exempt amounts that the defendant must be paid. If your answer covers more than one pay period, multiply the preceding amount by the number of pay periods and/or fraction thereof your answer covers. If you use a pay period not shown, prorate the monthly exempt amount.

Subtract the larger of lines 4 and 5 from line 3: $ _____ (6)

Enter amount (if any) withheld from this paycheck for on-going government liens such as child support: $ _____ (7)

Subtract line 7 from line 6. This amount must be held out for the plaintiff: $ _____ (8)
[CALCULATE THESE AMOUNTS TO DETERMINE THE AMOUNT TO WITHHOLD]
This is the formula that you will use for withholding each pay period over the required sixty-day garnishment period. Deduct any allowable processing fee you may charge from the amount that is to be paid to the defendant.

If there is any uncertainty about your answer give an explanation on the last page or on an attached page.

SECTION III: An attorney may answer for the garnishee.

Under penalty of perjury, I affirm that I have examined this answer, including accompanied schedules, and to the best of my knowledge and belief it is true, correct, and complete.

YOUR COMPANY NAME HERE
Signature of Garnishee Defendant

DATE YOU SIGNED
Date

YOUR SIGNATURE
Signature of person answering for Garnishee

YOUR TITLE
Connection with Garnishee

PRINT YOUR NAME
Print name of person signing

Address of Garnishee

If necessary, use this space to supplement your answer from the first and second pages:
[WRITE IN "SEE ATTACHED WORKSHEET" IF YOU USED ONE]

1st ANS TO WRIT OF GARN FOR CONT LIEN ON EARNINGS (ANWRGR) - Page 3 of 3
WPF GARN 01.0750 (06/2012) - RCW 6.27. 340

APPENDIX 5

ATTACHMENT TO ANSWER TO WRIT OF GARNISHMENT

Plaintiff/Creditor: _____

Defendant/Employee: _____

Garnishee/Employer: _____

Court/Case No.: _____

Date Writ Served: _____

Effective Dates: _____ to _____

Employee's Gross Earnings: $_____

Less Mandatory Deductions: $_____

Employee's Disposable Earnings: $_____

Less 75% Exempt Amount: $_____

Less Ongoing Liens/Child Support: $_____

      Amount Withheld: $_____

Other Property of Defendant/Employee in Garnishee/Employer's Possession at Time of Service of Writ:

_____

Notes: _____

APPENDIX 6

JUDGMENT ON ANSWER AND ORDER TO PAY

SUPERIOR COURT OF WASHINGTON
COUNTY OF KING

FRIENDLY FINANCE COMPANY

          Plaintiff,

vs.

RICK SMITH

          Defendant(s),

YOUR COMPANY

          Garnishee.

NO. 11-2-12345-6 XYZ

Judgment on **Answer and Order**
to Pay
(JDAGD)

I. JUDGMENT SUMMARY

Judgment Creditor:	Friendly Finance Company
Garnishment Judgment Debtor (Garnishee):	Your Company
Garnishment Judgment Amount:	$500.00
Costs Judgment Debtor (Defendant):	Rick Smith
Costs Judgment Amount (Costs and Attorneys' Fees):	$430.00
Judgments to Bear Interest at:	12 %
Attorney for Judgment Creditor:	John Doe Lawyer, WSBA #99999

II. BASIS

IT APPEARING THAT garnishee was indebted to defendant in the nonexempt amount of $ 500.00; that at the time the Writ of Garnishment was issued defendant was employed by or maintained a financial institution account with garnishee, or garnishee had in its possession or control funds, personal property, or effects of defendant; and that plaintiff has incurred recoverable costs and attorney fees of $430.00; now, therefore, it is hereby

III. ORDER

ORDERED that plaintiff is awarded judgment against garnishee in the amount of $500.00; that plaintiff is awarded judgment against defendant in the amount of $430.00 for recoverable costs;

    If this is a superior court order, garnishee shall pay its judgment amount to (check one)
    [ ] plaintiff [X] plaintiff's attorney through the registry of the court, and the clerk of the

JUDGMENT AND ORDER TO PAY (JDAGD) - Page 1 of 2
WPF GARN 01.0850 (06/2012) - RCW 4.64.030, 6.27.250

GARNISHMENT

court shall note receipt thereof and forthwith disburse such payment to (check one)
[ ] plaintiff [X] plaintiff's attorney

If this is a district court order, garnishee shall pay its judgment amount to (check one)
[ ] plaintiff [ ] plaintiff's attorney, and if any payment is received by the clerk of the court,
the clerk shall forthwith disburse such payment to [ ] plaintiff [ ] plaintiff's attorney.

[If payment is to be made directly to plaintiff, insert the following sentence: Any payment
directed to plaintiff shall be mailed to the following address: _____
_____.]

Garnishee is advised that the failure to pay its judgment amount may result in execution of the
judgment, including garnishment.

Dated: April 1, 2018 _____   /s/ WES T. WOOD _____
                                              JUDGE/COMMISSIONER

Court Address:

516 Third Avenue
Seattle, WA 98104

Presented by:

/s/ John Doe Lawyer
Plaintiff or Plaintiff's Attorney/WSBA No. 99999

APPENDIX 7

TITLE 6.27 RCW – GARNISHMENT

Portions of Washington's Garnishment statute, Chapter 6.27, Revised Code of Washington, effective as of June 1, 2018, are provided for reference. Because statutes are amended, repealed, or otherwise modified from time to time, you should always refer to the current statute before taking any action related to a writ of garnishment.

The current text of RCW 6.27 can be viewed at the Washington State Legislature's website:

http://app.leg.wa.gov/rcw/default.aspx?cite=6.27

6.27.005
Legislative intent.

The legislature recognizes that a garnishee has no responsibility for the situation leading to the garnishment of a debtor's wages, funds, or other property, but that the garnishment process is necessary for the enforcement of obligations debtors otherwise fail to honor, and that garnishment procedures benefit the state and the business community as creditors. The state should take whatever measures that are reasonably necessary to reduce or offset the administrative burden on the garnishee consistent with the goal of effectively enforcing the debtor's unpaid obligations.

[2000 c 72 § 1; 1998 c 227 § 1; 1997 c 296 § 1.]

6.27.010
Definitions.

(1) As used in this chapter, the term "earnings" means compensation paid or payable to an individual for personal services, whether denominated as wages, salary, commission, bonus, or otherwise, and includes periodic payments pursuant to a governmental or nongovernmental pension or retirement program.

(2) As used in this chapter, the term "disposable earnings" means that part of earnings remaining after the deduction from those earnings of any amounts required by law to be withheld.

[2012 c 159 § 1; 2003 c 222 § 16; 1987 c 442 § 1001.]

6.27.040
State and municipal corporations subject to garnishment—Service of writ.

(1) The state of Washington, all counties, cities, towns, school districts and other municipal corporations shall be subject to garnishment after judgment has been entered in the principal action, but not before, in the superior and district courts, in the same manner and with the same effect, as

provided in the case of other garnishees.

(2) The venue of any such garnishment proceeding shall be the same as for the original action, and the writ shall be issued by the clerk of the court having jurisdiction of such original action or by the attorney of record for the judgment creditor in district court.

(3) The writ of garnishment shall be served upon the same officer as is required for service of summons upon the commencement of a civil action against the state, county, city, town, school district, or other municipal corporation, as the case may be.

[2003 c 222 § 2. Prior: 1987 c 442 § 1004; 1987 c 202 § 134; 1969 ex.s. c 264 § 6. Formerly RCW 7.33.060.

6.27.050
Garnishment of money held by officer—Of judgment debtor—Of personal representative.

A sheriff or other peace officer who holds money of the defendant is subject to garnishment, excepting only for money or property taken from a person arrested by such officer, at the time of the arrest. A judgment debtor of the defendant is subject to garnishment when the judgment has not been previously assigned on the record or by writing filed in the office of the clerk of the court that entered the judgment and minuted by the clerk as an assignment in the execution docket. An executor or administrator is subject to garnishment for money due from the decedent to the defendant.

GARNISHMENT

[1987 c 442 § 1005; 1927 c 101 § 1; 1886 p 43 § 19; RRS § 664. Prior: Code 1881 §§ 174-192; 1877 pp 35-40; 1873 pp 43-50; 1871 pp 9, 10; 1869 pp 41-47; 1863 pp 112-120; 1860 pp 30-36; 1854 pp 155-162. Formerly RCW 7.12.180.

6.27.090
Amount garnishee required to hold.

(1) The writ of garnishment shall set forth in the first paragraph the amount that garnishee is required to hold, which shall be an amount determined as follows: (a)(i) If after judgment, the amount of the judgment remaining unsatisfied on the clerk of the court's execution docket, if any, plus interest to the date of garnishment, as provided in RCW 4.56.110, plus estimated interest that may accrue during the garnishment process on a per diem basis under subsection (3) of this section plus taxable costs and attorneys' fees, or (ii) if before judgment, the amount prayed for in the complaint plus estimated taxable costs of suit and attorneys' fees, together with, (b) whether before or after judgment, estimated costs of garnishment as provided in subsection (2) of this section. The court may, by order, set a higher amount to be held upon a showing of good cause by plaintiff.

(2) Costs recoverable in garnishment proceedings, to be estimated for purposes of subsection (1) of this section, include filing and ex parte fees, service and affidavit fees, postage and costs of certified mail, answer fee or fees, other fees legally chargeable to a plaintiff in the garnishment process, and a garnishment attorney fee in the amount of the

greater of one hundred dollars or ten percent of (a) the amount of the judgment remaining unsatisfied or (b) the amount prayed for in the complaint. The garnishment attorney fee shall not exceed three hundred dollars.

(3) For purposes of subsection (1) of this section, the plaintiff must indicate in the writ a specific dollar amount of estimated interest that may accrue during the garnishment process per day. The amount must be based on an interest rate of twelve percent or the interest rate set forth in the judgment, whichever rate is less.

[2012 c 159 § 2; 2000 c 72 § 2; 1988 c 231 § 24; 1987 c 442 § 1009; 1969 ex.s. c 264 § 9. Formerly RCW 7.33.090.

6.27.095
Garnishee's processing fees.

(1) The garnishee of a writ for a continuing lien on earnings may deduct a processing fee from the remainder of the obligor's earnings after withholding the required amount under the writ. The processing fee may not exceed twenty dollars for the first answer and ten dollars at the time the garnishee submits the second answer.

(2) If the writ of garnishment is not a writ for a continuing lien on earnings, the garnishee is entitled to check or money order payable to the garnishee in the amount of twenty dollars at the time the writ of garnishment is served on the garnishee as required under RCW 6.27.110(1).

[1998 c 227 § 2; 1997 c 296 § 3.]

6.27.110

Service of writ generally—Forms—Requirements for person serving writ—Return.

(1) Service of the writ of garnishment, including a writ for continuing lien on earnings, on the garnishee is invalid unless the writ is served together with: (a) An answer form as prescribed in RCW 6.27.190; and (b) a check or money order made payable to the garnishee in the amount of twenty dollars for the answer fee if the writ of garnishment is not a writ for a continuing lien on earnings.

(2) Except as provided in RCW 6.27.080 for service on a bank, savings and loan association, or credit union, the writ of garnishment shall be mailed to the garnishee by certified mail, return receipt requested, addressed in the same manner as a summons in a civil action, and will be binding upon the garnishee on the day set forth on the return receipt. In the alternative, the writ shall be served by the sheriff of the county in which the garnishee lives or has its place of business or by any person qualified to serve process in the same manner as a summons in a civil action is served.

(3) If a writ of garnishment is served by a sheriff, the sheriff shall file with the clerk of the court that issued the writ a signed return showing the time, place, and manner of service and that the writ was accompanied by an answer form, and check or money order if required by this section, and noting thereon fees for making the service. If service is made by any person other than a sheriff, such person shall file an affidavit including

the same information and showing qualifications to make such service. If a writ of garnishment is served by mail, the person making the mailing shall file an affidavit showing the time, place, and manner of mailing and that the writ was accompanied by an answer form, and check or money order if required by this section, and shall attach the return receipt or electronic return receipt delivery confirmation to the affidavit.

[2012 c 159 § 6; 1998 c 227 § 4; 1997 c 296 § 4; 1988 c 231 § 26; 1987 c 442 § 1011; 1981 c 193 § 5; 1971 ex.s. c 292 § 8; 1970 ex.s. c 61 § 11; 1969 ex.s. c 264 § 13.Formerly RCW 7.33.130.

6.27.120
Effect of service of writ.

(1) From and after the service of a writ of garnishment, it shall not be lawful, except as provided in this chapter or as directed by the court, for the garnishee to pay any debt owing to the defendant at the time of such service, or to deliver, sell or transfer, or recognize any sale or transfer of, any personal property or effects belonging to the defendant in the garnishee's possession or under the garnishee's control at the time of such service; and any such payment, delivery, sale or transfer shall be void and of no effect as to so much of said debt, personal property or effects as may be necessary to satisfy the plaintiff's demand.

(2) This section shall have no effect as to any portion of a debt that is exempt from garnishment.

(3) The garnishee shall incur no liability for releasing funds or property in excess of the amount stated in the writ of garnishment if the garnishee continues to hold an amount equal to the amount stated in the writ of garnishment.

[1987 c 442 § 1012; 1969 ex.s. c 264 § 14. Formerly RCW 7.33.140.

6.27.130

Mailing of writ and judgment or affidavit to judgment debtor—Mailing of notice and claim form if judgment debtor is an individual—Service—Return.

(1) When a writ is issued under a judgment, on or before the date of service of the writ on the garnishee, the judgment creditor shall mail or cause to be mailed to the judgment debtor, by certified mail, addressed to the last known post office address of the judgment debtor, (a) a copy of the writ and a copy of the judgment creditor's affidavit submitted in application for the writ, and (b) if the judgment debtor is an individual, the notice and claim form prescribed in RCW6.27.140. In the alternative, on or before the day of the service of the writ on the garnishee or within two days thereafter, the stated documents shall be served on the judgment debtor in the same manner as is required for personal service of summons upon a party to an action.

(2) The requirements of this section shall not be jurisdictional, but (a) no disbursement order or judgment

against the garnishee defendant shall be entered unless there is on file the return or affidavit of service or mailing required by subsection (3) of this section, and (b) if the copies of the writ and judgment or affidavit, and the notice and claim form if the defendant is an individual, are not mailed or served as herein provided, or if any irregularity appears with respect to the mailing or service, the court, in its discretion, on motion of the judgment debtor promptly made and supported by affidavit showing that the judgment debtor has suffered substantial injury from the plaintiff's failure to mail or otherwise to serve such copies, may set aside the garnishment and award to the judgment debtor an amount equal to the damages suffered because of such failure.

(3) If the service on the judgment debtor is made by a sheriff, the sheriff shall file with the clerk of the court that issued the writ a signed return showing the time, place, and manner of service and that the copy of the writ was accompanied by a copy of a judgment or affidavit, and by a notice and claim form if required by this section, and shall note thereon fees for making such service. If service is made by any person other than a sheriff, such person shall file an affidavit including the same information and showing qualifications to make such service. If service on the judgment debtor is made by mail, the person making the mailing shall file an affidavit including the same information as required for return on service and, in addition, showing the address of the mailing and attaching the return receipt or the mailing should it be returned to the sender as undeliverable.

[2003 c 222 § 5; 1988 c 231 § 27; 1987 c 442 § 1013; 1969 ex.s. c 264 § 32. Formerly RCW 7.33.320.

6.27.150

Exemption of earnings—Amount.

*** CHANGE IN 2018 *** (SEE 1169-S3.SL) ***

(1) Except as provided in subsection (2) of this section, if the garnishee is an employer owing the defendant earnings, then for each week of such earnings, an amount shall be exempt from garnishment which is the greatest of the following:

(a) Thirty-five times the federal minimum hourly wage in effect at the time the earnings are payable; or

(b) Seventy-five percent of the disposable earnings of the defendant.

(2) In the case of a garnishment based on a judgment or other order for child support or court order for spousal maintenance, other than a mandatory wage assignment order pursuant to chapter 26.18 RCW, or a mandatory assignment of retirement benefits pursuant to chapter 41.50 RCW, the exemption shall be fifty percent of the disposable earnings of the defendant.

(3) The exemptions stated in this section shall apply whether such earnings are paid, or are to be paid, weekly, monthly, or at other intervals, and whether earnings are due the defendant for one week, a portion thereof, or for a longer period.

(4) Unless directed otherwise by the court, the garnishee

shall determine and deduct exempt amounts under this section as directed in the writ of garnishment and answer, and shall pay these amounts to the defendant.

(5) No money due or earned as earnings as defined in RCW 6.27.010 shall be exempt from garnishment under the provisions of RCW 6.15.010, as now or hereafter amended.

[2012 c 159 § 9; 1991 c 365 § 26; 1987 c 442 § 1015; 1981 c 193 § 6; 1971 c 6 § 1; 1970 ex.s. c 61 § 3; 1969 ex.s. c 264 § 28. Formerly RCW 7.33.280.

6.27.160

Claiming exemptions—Form—Hearing—Attorney's fees—Costs—Release of funds or property.

(1) A defendant may claim exemptions from garnishment in the manner specified by the statute that creates the exemption or by delivering to or mailing by first-class mail to the clerk of the court out of which the writ was issued a declaration in substantially the following form or in the form set forth in RCW 6.27.140and mailing a copy of the form by first-class mail to the plaintiff or plaintiff's attorney at the address shown on the writ of garnishment, all not later than twenty-eight days after the date stated on the writ except that the time shall be extended to allow a declaration mailed or delivered to the clerk within twenty-one days after service of the writ on the garnishee if service on the garnishee is delayed more than seven days after the date of the writ.

[Form omitted; refer to statute.

(2) A plaintiff who wishes to object to an exemption claim must, not later than seven days after receipt of the claim, cause to be delivered or mailed to the defendant by first-class mail, to the address shown on the exemption claim, a declaration by self, attorney, or agent, alleging the facts on which the objection is based, together with notice of date, time, and place of a hearing on the objection, which hearing the plaintiff must cause to be noted for a hearing date not later than fourteen days after the receipt of the claim. After a hearing on an objection to an exemption claim, the court shall award costs to the prevailing party and may also award an attorney's fee to the prevailing party if the court concludes that the exemption claim or the objection to the claim was not made in good faith. The defendant bears the burden of proving any claimed exemption, including the obligation to provide sufficient documentation to identify the source and amount of any claimed exempt funds.

(3) If the plaintiff elects not to object to the claim of exemption, the plaintiff shall, not later than ten days after receipt of the claim, obtain from the court and deliver to the garnishee an order directing the garnishee to release such part of the debt, property, or effects as is covered by the exemption claim. If the plaintiff fails to obtain and deliver the order as required or otherwise to effect release of the exempt funds or property, the defendant shall be entitled to recover fifty dollars from the plaintiff, in addition to actual damages suffered by the defendant from the failure to release the exempt property. The attorney of record for the plaintiff may, as an alternative to obtaining a court order releasing exempt funds, property, or

effects, deliver to the garnishee and file with the court an authorization to release claimed exempt funds, property, or effects, signed by the attorney...

[Form omitted; refer to statute.

6.27.170

Garnished employee not to be discharged— Exception.

No employer shall discharge an employee for the reason that a creditor of the employee has subjected or attempted to subject unpaid earnings of the employee to a writ of garnishment directed to the employer: PROVIDED, HOWEVER, That this provision shall not apply if garnishments on three or more separate indebtednesses are served upon the employer within any period of twelve consecutive months.

[1987 c 442 § 1017; 1969 ex.s. c 264 § 16. Formerly RCW 7.33.160.

6.27.190

Answer of garnishee—Contents—Forms.

(1) The answer of the garnishee shall be signed by the garnishee or attorney or if the garnishee is a corporation, by an officer, attorney or duly authorized agent of the garnishee, under penalty of perjury, and the original and copies delivered, either personally or by mail, as instructed in the writ.

(2) If the writ of garnishment is for a continuing lien, the answer forms shall be as prescribed in RCW 6.27.340 and 6.27.350.

(3) If the writ is not directed to an employer for the purpose of garnishing the defendant's wages, the answer shall be substantially in the following form:

[Form omitted; refer to statute.

[2012 c 159 § 10; 2003 c 222 § 8; 2000 c 72 § 4; 1997 c 296 § 5; 1988 c 231 § 30; 1987 c 442 § 1019; 1969 ex.s. c 264 § 15. Formerly RCW 7.33.150.

6.27.200

Default judgment—Reduction upon motion of garnishee—Attorney's fees.

If the garnishee fails to answer the writ within the time prescribed in the writ, after the time to answer the writ has expired and after required returns or affidavits have been filed, showing service on the garnishee and service on or mailing to the defendant, it shall be lawful for the court to render judgment by default against such garnishee, after providing a notice to the garnishee by personal service or first-class mail deposited in the mail at least ten calendar days prior to entry of the judgment, for the full amount claimed by the plaintiff against the defendant, or in case the plaintiff has a judgment against the defendant, for the full amount of the plaintiff's unpaid judgment against the defendant with all accruing interest and costs as prescribed in RCW 6.27.090: PROVIDED,

That upon motion by the garnishee at any time within seven days following service on, or mailing to, the garnishee of a copy of the first writ of execution or writ of garnishment under such judgment, the judgment against the garnishee shall be reduced to the amount of any nonexempt funds or property which was actually in the possession of the garnishee at the time the writ was served, plus the cumulative amount of the nonexempt earnings subject to the lien provided for in RCW6.27.350, or the sum of one hundred dollars, whichever is more, but in no event to exceed the full amount claimed by the plaintiff or the amount of the unpaid judgment against the principal defendant with all accruing interest and costs and attorney's fees as prescribed in RCW 6.27.090, plus the accruing interest and costs and attorneys' fees as prescribed in RCW 6.27.090 for any garnishment on the judgment against the garnishee, and in addition the plaintiff shall be entitled to a reasonable attorney's fee for the plaintiff's response to the garnishee's motion to reduce said judgment against the garnishee under this proviso and the court may allow additional attorney's fees for other actions taken because of the garnishee's failure to answer.

[2012 c 159 § 11; 2003 c 222 § 9; 1997 c 296 § 6; 1988 c 231 § 31; 1987 c 442 § 1020; 1970 ex.s. c 61 § 10; 1969 ex.s. c 264 § 19. Formerly RCW 7.33.190.

6.27.210

Answer of garnishee may be controverted by plaintiff or defendant.

If the garnishee files an answer, either the plaintiff or the defendant, if not satisfied with the answer of the garnishee, may controvert within twenty days after the filing of the answer, by filing an affidavit in writing signed by the controverting party or attorney or agent, stating that the affiant has good reason to believe and does believe that the answer of the garnishee is incorrect, stating in what particulars the affiant believes the same is incorrect. Copies of the affidavit shall be served on or mailed by first-class mail to the garnishee at the address indicated on the answer or, if no address is indicated, at the address to or at which the writ was mailed or served, and to the other party, at the address shown on the writ if the defendant controverts, or at the address to or at which the copy of the writ of garnishment was mailed or served on the defendant if the plaintiff controverts, unless otherwise directed in writing by the defendant or defendant's attorney.

[1987 c 442 § 1021; 1969 ex.s. c 264 § 24. Formerly RCW 7.33.240.

6.27.220

Controversion—Procedure.

If the answer of the garnishee is controverted, as provided in RCW 6.27.210, the garnishee may respond by affidavit of the garnishee, the garnishee's attorney or agent, within twenty days of the filing of the controverting affidavit, with copies served on or mailed by first-class mail to the plaintiff at the address shown on the writ and to the defendant as provided in

RCW 6.27.210. Upon the expiration of the time for garnishee's response, the matter may be noted by any party for hearing before a commissioner or presiding judge for a determination whether an issue is presented that requires a trial. If a trial is required, it shall be noted as in other cases, but no pleadings shall be necessary on such issue other than the affidavit of the plaintiff, the answer of the garnishee and the reply of the plaintiff or defendant controverting such answer, unless otherwise ordered by the court.

[1987 c 442 § 1022; 1969 ex.s. c 264 § 26. Formerly RCW 7.33.260.

6.27.230
Controversion—Costs and attorney's fees.

Where the answer is controverted, the costs of the proceeding, including a reasonable compensation for attorney's fees, shall be awarded to the prevailing party: PROVIDED, That no costs or attorney's fees in such contest shall be taxable to the defendant in the event of a controversion by the plaintiff.

[1987 c 442 § 1023; 1969 ex.s. c 264 § 29. Formerly RCW 7.33.290.

6.27.240
Discharge of garnishee.

If it appears from the answer of the garnishee that the

garnishee was not indebted to the defendant when the writ of garnishment was served, and that the garnishee did not have possession or control of any personal property or effects of the defendant, and if an affidavit controverting the answer of the garnishee is not filed within twenty days of the filing of the answer, as provided in this chapter, the garnishee shall stand discharged without further action by the court or the garnishee and shall have no further liability.

[1987 c 442 § 1024; 1969 ex.s. c 264 § 18. Formerly RCW 7.33.180.

6.27.250

Judgment against garnishee—Procedure if debt not mature.

(1)(a) If it appears from the answer of the garnishee or if it is otherwise made to appear that the garnishee was indebted to the defendant in any amount, not exempt, when the writ of garnishment was served, and if the required return or affidavit showing service on or mailing to the defendant is on file, the court shall render judgment for the plaintiff against such garnishee for the amount so admitted or found to be due to the defendant from the garnishee, unless such amount exceeds the amount of the plaintiff's claim or judgment against the defendant with accruing interest and costs and attorney's fees as prescribed in RCW 6.27.090, in which case it shall be for the amount of such claim or judgment, with said interest, costs, and fees. If there is no unresolved exemption claim and no controversion, the plaintiff may apply for the judgment and order to pay ex parte. In the case of a superior court garnishment, the court shall order the garnishee to pay to the plaintiff or to the plaintiff's attorney through the registry of the court the amount of the judgment against the garnishee, the clerk of the court shall note receipt of any such payment, and the clerk of the court shall disburse the payment to the plaintiff. In the case of a district court garnishment, the court shall order the garnishee to pay the judgment amount directly to the plaintiff or to the plaintiff's attorney. In either case, the court shall inform the garnishee that failure to pay the amount may result in execution of the judgment, including garnishment.

(b) If, prior to judgment, the garnishee tenders to the plaintiff or to the plaintiff's attorney or to the court any amounts due, such tender will support judgment against the garnishee in the amount so tendered, subject to any exemption claimed within the time required in RCW 6.27.160 after the amounts are tendered, and subject to any controversion filed within the time required in RCW 6.27.210 after the amounts are tendered. Any amounts tendered to the court by or on behalf of the garnishee or the defendant prior to judgment shall be disbursed to the party entitled to same upon entry of judgment or order, and any amounts so tendered after entry of judgment or order shall be disbursed upon receipt to the party entitled to same.

(2) If it shall appear from the answer of the garnishee and the same is not controverted, or if it shall appear from the hearing or trial on controversion or by stipulation of the parties that the garnishee is indebted to the principal defendant in any sum, but that such indebtedness is not matured and is not due

and payable, and if the required return or affidavit showing service on or mailing to the defendant is on file, the court shall make an order requiring the garnishee to pay such sum into court when the same becomes due, the date when such payment is to be made to be specified in the order, and in default thereof that judgment shall be entered against the garnishee for the amount of such indebtedness so admitted or found due. In case the garnishee pays the sum at the time specified in the order, the payment shall operate as a discharge, otherwise judgment shall be entered against the garnishee for the amount of such indebtedness, which judgment shall have the same force and effect, and be enforced in the same manner as other judgments entered against garnishees as provided in this chapter: PROVIDED, That if judgment is rendered in favor of the principal defendant, or if any judgment rendered against the principal defendant is satisfied prior to the date of payment specified in an order of payment entered under this subsection, the garnishee shall not be required to make the payment, nor shall any judgment in such case be entered against the garnishee.

(3) The court shall, upon request of the plaintiff at the time judgment is rendered against the garnishee or within one year thereafter, or within one year after service of the writ on the garnishee if no judgment is taken against the garnishee, render judgment against the defendant for recoverable garnishment costs and attorney fees. However, if it appears from the answer of garnishee or otherwise that, at the time the writ was issued, the garnishee held no funds, personal property, or effects of the defendant and, in the case of a garnishment on earnings, the defendant was not employed by the garnishee,

or, in the case of a writ directed to a financial institution, the defendant maintained no account therein, then the plaintiff may not be awarded judgment against the defendant for such costs or attorney fees.

[2012 c 159 § 12; 2003 c 222 § 10; 2000 c 72 § 5; 1988 c 231 § 32; 1987 c 442 § 1025; 1969 ex.s. c 264 § 20. Formerly RCW 7.33.200.

6.27.260
Execution on judgment against garnishee.

Execution may be issued on the judgment against the garnishee in the same manner as upon any other judgment. The amount made upon any such execution shall be paid by the officer executing it to the clerk of the court from which the execution was issued; and, in cases where judgment has been rendered against the defendant, the amount made on the execution shall be applied to the satisfaction of the judgment, interest and costs against the defendant. In case judgment has not been rendered against the defendant at the time execution issued against the garnishee is returned, any amount made on the execution shall be paid to the clerk of the court from which the execution issued, who shall retain the same until judgment is rendered in the action between the plaintiff and defendant. In case judgment is rendered in favor of the plaintiff, the amount made on the execution against the garnishee shall be applied to the satisfaction of such judgment and the surplus, if any, shall be paid to the defendant. In case judgment is rendered in favor of the defendant, the amount made on the execution against the garnishee shall be paid to the defendant.

[1987 c 442 § 1026; 1969 ex.s. c 264 § 21. Formerly RCW 7.33.210.

6.27.265

Form for judgment against garnishee.

The judgment on garnishee's answer or tendered funds, and for costs against defendant, and the order to pay funds shall be substantially in the following form:

[Form omitted; refer to statute.

[2003 c 222 § 11; 2000 c 72 § 6.]

6.27.270

Decree directing garnishee to deliver up effects—Disposition.

If it appears from the garnishee's answer or otherwise that the garnishee had possession or control, when the writ was served, of any personal property or effects of the defendant liable to execution, and if the required return or affidavit showing service on or mailing to the defendant is on file, the court shall render a decree requiring the garnishee to deliver up to the sheriff on demand, and after making arrangements with the sheriff as to time and place of delivery, such personal property or effects or so much of them as may be necessary to satisfy the plaintiff's claim. If a judgment has been rendered in favor of the plaintiff against the defendant, such personal property or effects may be sold in the same manner as any other property is sold upon an execution issued on said judgment. If judgment has not been rendered in the principal action, the sheriff shall retain possession of the personal property or effects until the rendition of judgment therein, and, if judgment is thereafter rendered in favor of the plaintiff, said personal property or effects, or sufficient of them to satisfy such judgment, may be sold in the same manner as other property is sold on execution, by virtue of an execution issued on the judgment in the principal action. If judgment is rendered in the action against the plaintiff and in favor of the defendant, such effects and personal property shall be returned to the defendant by the sheriff: PROVIDED, HOWEVER, That if such effects or personal property are of a perishable nature, or the interests of the parties will be subserved by making a sale thereof before judgment, the court may order a sale thereof by the sheriff in the same manner as sales upon execution are made, and the proceeds of such sale shall be paid to the clerk of the court that issued the writ, and the same disposition shall be made of the proceeds at the termination of the action as would have been made of the personal property or effects under the provisions of this section in case the sale had not been made.

[1988 c 231 § 33; 1987 c 442 § 1027; 1969 ex.s. c 264 § 22. Formerly RCW 7.33.220.

6.27.280

Procedure upon failure of garnishee to deliver.

If the garnishee, adjudged to have effects or personal property of the defendant in possession or under control as provided in RCW 6.27.270, fails or refuses to deliver them to the sheriff on such demand, the officer shall immediately make return of such failure or refusal, whereupon, on motion of the plaintiff, the garnishee shall be cited to show cause why he or she should not be found in contempt of court for such failure or refusal, and should the garnishee fail to show some good and sufficient excuse for such failure and refusal, he or she shall be fined for such contempt and imprisoned until he or she shall deliver such personal property or effects.

[1987 c 442 § 1028; 1969 ex.s. c 264 § 23. Formerly RCW 7.33.230.

6.27.290

Similarity of names—Procedure.

(1) If the garnishee in the answer states that the garnishee at the time of the service of the writ was indebted to or had possession or control of personal property or effects belonging to a person with a name the same as or similar to the name of the defendant, and stating the place of business or residence of said person, and that the garnishee does not know whether or not such person is the same person as the defendant, and prays the court to determine whether or not the person is the same person as the defendant, the court, before rendering judgment against the garnishee defendant as hereinbefore

provided, shall conduct a hearing to take proof as to the identity of said persons.

(2) Before the hearing on the question of identity, the plaintiff shall cause the court to issue a citation directed to the person identified in the garnishee's answer, commanding that person to appear before the court from which the citation is issued within ten days after the service of the same, and to answer on oath whether or not he or she is the same person as the defendant in said action. The citation shall be dated and attested in the same manner as a writ of garnishment and be delivered to the plaintiff or the plaintiff's attorney and shall be served in the same manner as a summons in a civil action is served.

(3) If the court finds after hearing that the persons are not the same, the garnishee shall be discharged and shall recover costs against the plaintiff. If the court finds that the persons are the same, it shall make the same kind of judgment as in other cases in which the garnishee is held upon the garnishee's answer, including provision for garnishee's costs.

(4) If the court finds after the hearing that the defendant or judgment debtor is the same person as the person identified in the garnishee's answer, it shall be sufficient answer to any claim of said person against the garnishee founded on any indebtedness of the garnishee or on the possession or control by the garnishee of any personal property or effects for the garnishee to show that the indebtedness was paid or the personal property or effects were delivered under the judgment of the court in accordance with the provisions in this chapter.

[1987 c 442 § 1029; 1969 ex.s. c 264 § 33. Formerly RCW 7.33.330.

6.27.300

Garnishee protected against claim of defendant.

It shall be a sufficient answer to any claim of the defendant against the garnishee founded on any indebtedness of the garnishee or on the possession or control by the garnishee of any personal property or effects, for the garnishee to show that such indebtedness was paid or such personal property or effects were delivered under the judgment of the court in accordance with this chapter.

[1987 c 442 § 1030; 1969 ex.s. c 264 § 30. Formerly RCW 7.33.300.

6.27.310

Dismissal of writ after one year—Notice—Exception.

In all cases where it shall appear from the answer of the garnishee that the garnishee was indebted to the defendant when the writ of garnishment was served, no controversion is pending, there has been no discharge or judgment against the garnishee entered, and one year has passed since the filing of the answer of the garnishee, the court, after ten days' notice in writing to the plaintiff, shall enter an order dismissing the writ of garnishment and discharging the garnishee: PROVIDED, That this provision shall have no effect if the cause of action between plaintiff and defendant is pending on the trial calendar, or if any party files an affidavit that the action is still pending.

[1987 c 442 § 1031; 1969 ex.s. c 264 § 27. Formerly RCW 7.33.270.

6.27.320
Dismissal of garnishment—Duty of plaintiff— Procedure—Penalty—Costs.

In any case where garnishee has answered that it is holding funds or property belonging to defendant and plaintiff shall obtain satisfaction of the judgment and payment of recoverable garnishment costs and attorney fees from a source other than the garnishment, upon written demand of the defendant or the garnishee, it shall be the duty of plaintiff to obtain an order dismissing the garnishment and to serve it upon the garnishee within twenty days after the demand or the satisfaction of judgment and payment of costs and fees, whichever shall be later. The attorney of record for the plaintiff may, as an alternative to obtaining a court order dismissing the garnishment, deliver to the garnishee and file with the court an authorization to dismiss the garnishment in whole or part, signed by the attorney, in substantially the form indicated in RCW 6.27.160(3). In the event of the failure of plaintiff to obtain and serve such an order or release, if garnishee continues to hold such funds or property, defendant shall be entitled to move for dismissal of the garnishment and shall further be entitled to a judgment against plaintiff of one hundred dollars plus defendant's costs and damages. Dismissal may be on ex parte motion of the plaintiff.

[2003 c 222 § 12; 2000 c 72 § 7; 1969 ex.s. c 264 § 31. Formerly RCW 7.33.310.

6.27.330

Continuing lien on earnings—Authorized.

A judgment creditor may obtain a continuing lien on earnings by a garnishment pursuant to this chapter.

[2012 c 159 § 13; 1987 c 442 § 1032; 1970 ex.s. c 61 § 5. Formerly RCW 7.33.350.

6.27.340

Continuing lien on earnings—Forms for answer to writ.

(1) Service of a writ for a continuing lien shall comply fully with RCW 6.27.110.

(2) If the writ is directed to an employer for the purpose of garnishing the defendant's wages, the first answer shall accurately state, as of the date the writ of garnishment was issued as indicated by the date appearing on the last page of the writ, whether the defendant was employed by the garnishee defendant (and if not the date employment terminated), whether the defendant's earnings were subject to

a preexisting writ of garnishment for continuing liens on earnings (and if so the date such writ will terminate and the current writ will be enforced), whether the defendant maintained a financial account with garnishee, and whether the garnishee defendant had possession of or control over any funds, personal property, or effects of the defendant (and if so the garnishee defendant shall list all of defendant's personal property or effects in its possession or control). The first answer shall further accurately state, as of the time of service of the writ of garnishment on the garnishee defendant, the amount due and owing from the garnishee defendant to the defendant, and the defendant's total earnings, allowable deductions, disposable earnings, exempt earnings, deductions for superior liens such as child support, and net earnings withheld under the writ. The first answer may be substantially in the following form:

[Form omitted; see Appendix 4.

(3) Prior to serving the answer forms for a writ for continuing lien on earnings, the plaintiff shall fill in the minimum exemption amounts for the different pay periods, and the maximum percentages of disposable earnings subject to lien and exempt from lien.

(4) In the event plaintiff fails to comply with this section, employer may elect to treat the garnishment as one not creating a continuing lien.

[2012 c 159 § 5; 2003 c 222 § 13; 1988 c 231 § 34; 1987 c 442 § 1033; 1970 ex.s. c 61 § 6. Formerly RCW 7.33.360.

6.27.350

Continuing lien on earnings—When lien becomes effective—Termination—Second answer.

(1) Where the garnishee's answer to a garnishment for a continuing lien reflects that the defendant is employed by the garnishee, the judgment or balance due thereon as reflected on the writ of garnishment shall become a lien on earnings due at the time of the effective date of the writ, as defined in this subsection, to the extent that they are not exempt from garnishment, and such lien shall continue as to subsequent nonexempt earnings until the total subject to the lien equals the amount stated on the writ of garnishment or until the expiration of the employer's payroll period ending on or before sixty days after the effective date of the writ, whichever occurs first, except that such lien on subsequent earnings shall terminate sooner if the employment relationship is terminated or if the underlying judgment is vacated, modified, or satisfied in full or if the writ is dismissed. The "effective date" of a writ is the date of service of the writ if there is no previously served writ; otherwise, it is the date of termination of a previously served writ or writs.

(2) At the time of the expected termination of the lien, the plaintiff shall mail to the garnishee one copy of the answer form prescribed in RCW 6.27.340. The plaintiff shall replace the text of section I of the answer form with a statement in

substantially the following form: "ANSWER SECTION II OF THIS FORM WITH RESPECT TO THE TOTAL AMOUNT OF EARNINGS WITHHELD UNDER THIS GARNISHMENT, INCLUDING THE AMOUNT, IF ANY, STATED IN YOUR FIRST ANSWER, AND WITHIN TWENTY DAYS AFTER YOU RECEIVE THESE FORMS, MAIL OR DELIVER THEM AS DIRECTED IN THE WRIT."

Nonexempt amount due and owing stated in first answer	$ . . .
Nonexempt amount accrued since first answer	$ . . .
TOTAL AMOUNT WITHHELD	$. . . .

(3) Within twenty days of receipt of the second answer form the garnishee shall file a second answer, either in the form as provided in subsection (2) of this section, stating the total amount held subject to the garnishment, or otherwise containing the information required in subsection (2) of this section and a calculation indicating the total amount due and owing from the garnishee defendant to the defendant, the defendant's total earnings, allowable deductions, disposable earnings, exempt earnings, deductions for superior liens such as child support, and net earnings withheld under the writ.

[2012 c 159 § 14; 2003 c 222 § 14; 1997 c 296 § 7; 1988 c 231 § 35; 1987 c 442 § 1034; 1970 ex.s. c 61 § 7. Formerly RCW 7.33.370.

6.27.360

Continuing lien on earnings—Priorities— Exceptions.

(1) Except as provided in subsection (3) of this section, a lien obtained under RCW 6.27.350 shall have priority over any subsequent garnishment lien or wage assignment except that service of a writ shall not be effective to create a continuing lien with such priority if a writ in the same case is pending at the time of the service of the new writ.

(2) A lien obtained under RCW 6.27.350 shall have priority over any prior wage assignment, except an assignment for child support as provided in subsection (3) of this section and an assignment for legal financial obligations as provided under RCW 9.94A.760, 9.94A.7702, and 72.09.111.

(3) A lien obtained under RCW 6.27.350 shall not have priority over a notice of payroll deduction issued under RCW 26.23.060 or a wage assignment or other garnishment for child support issued under chapters 26.18 and 74.20A RCW. Should nonexempt wages remain after deduction of all amounts owing under a notice of payroll deduction, wage assignment, or garnishment for child support, the garnishee shall withhold the remaining nonexempt wages under the lien obtained under RCW 6.27.350.

[2012 c 159 § 15; 1997 c 296 § 8; 1989 c 360 § 20; 1987 c 442 § 1035; 1970 ex.s. c 61 § 8. Formerly RCW 7.33.380.

6.27.370

Notice to federal government as garnishee defendant—Deposit, payment, and endorsement of funds received by the clerk—Fees as recoverable cost.

(1) Whenever the federal government is named as a garnishee defendant, the attorney for the plaintiff, or the clerk of the court shall, upon submitting a notice in the appropriate form by the plaintiff, issue a notice which directs the garnishee defendant to disburse any nonexempt earnings to the court in accordance with the garnishee defendant's normal pay and disbursement cycle.

(2) Funds received by the clerk from a garnishee defendant may be deposited into the registry of the court or, in the case of negotiable instruments, may be retained in the court file. Upon presentation of an order directing the clerk to disburse the funds received, the clerk shall pay or endorse the funds over to the party entitled to receive the funds. Except for good cause shown, the funds shall not be paid or endorsed to the plaintiff prior to the expiration of any minimum statutory period allowed to the defendant for filing an exemption claim.

(3) The plaintiff shall, in the same manner permitted for service of the writ of garnishment, provide to the garnishee defendant a copy of the notice issued under subsection (1) of this section, and shall supply to the garnished party a copy of the notice.

(4) Any answer or processing fees charged by the garnishee defendant to the plaintiff under federal law shall be a

recoverable cost under RCW 6.27.090.

(5) The notice to the federal government garnishee shall be in substantially the following form:

[Form omitted; refer to statute.

(6) If the writ of garnishment is issued by the attorney of record for the judgment creditor, the following paragraph shall replace the clerk's signature and date:

> This notice is issued by the undersigned attorney of record for plaintiff under the authority of RCW 6.27.370, and must be complied with in the same manner as a notice issued by the court.

Dated this . . . . .day of . . . ., 20 . . . . . .

. . . .

Attorney for Plaintiff

[2012 c 159 § 16; 1997 c 296 § 9.]

6.27.900

Construction—Chapter applicable to state registered domestic partnerships—2009 c 521.

For the purposes of this chapter, the terms spouse, marriage, marital, husband, wife, widow, widower, next of kin, and family shall be interpreted as applying equally to state registered domestic partnerships or individuals in state registered domestic partnerships as well as to marital relationships and married persons, and references to dissolution of marriage shall apply equally to state registered domestic partnerships that have been terminated, dissolved, or invalidated, to the extent that such interpretation does not conflict with federal law. Where necessary to implement chapter 521, Laws of 2009, gender-specific terms such as husband and wife used in any statute, rule, or other law shall be construed to be gender neutral, and applicable to individuals in state registered domestic partnerships.

[2009 c 521 § 14.]

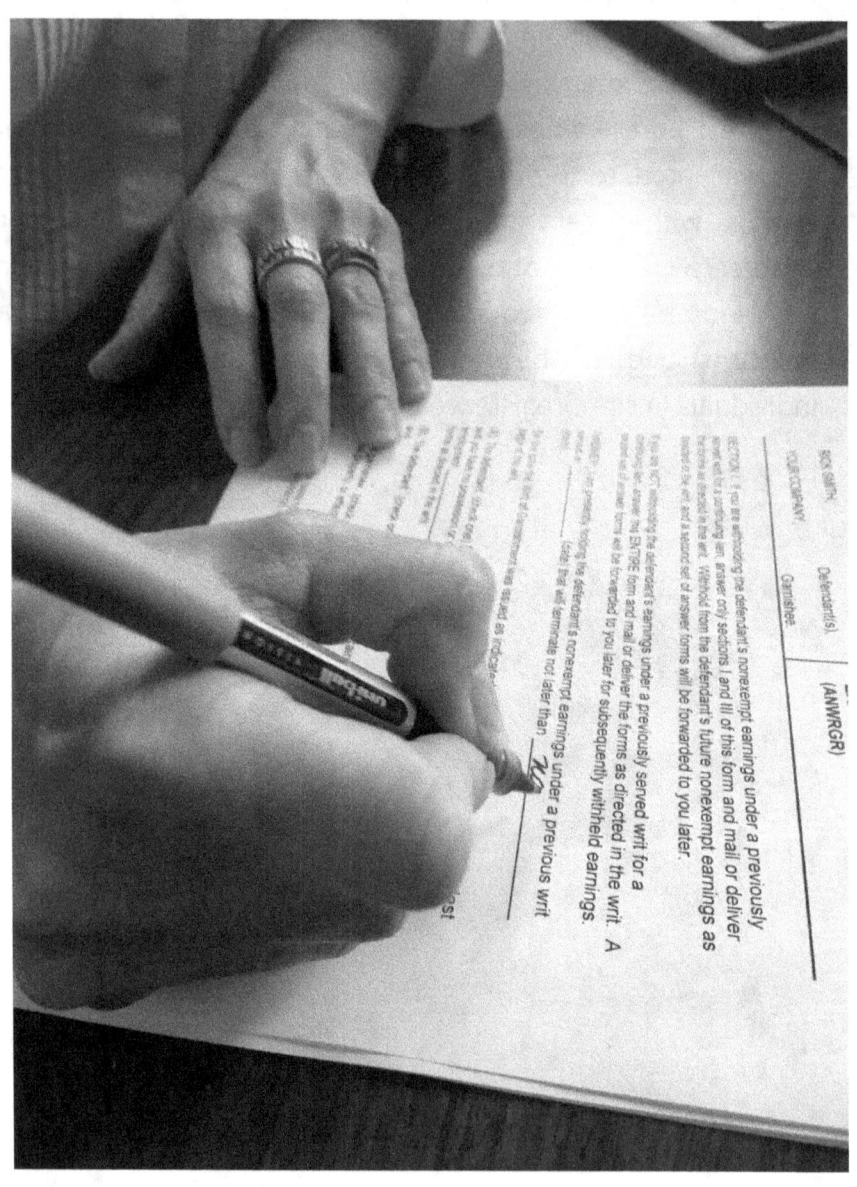

OTHER RESOURCES

Washington Department of Financial Management Chapter 25.60—Garnishments and Wage Assigments:

https://www.ofm.wa.gov/sites/default/files/public/legacy/policy/25.60.htm

Washington Department of Financial Management Payroll Resources:

https://www.ofm.wa.gov/accounting/administrative-accounting-resources/payroll

Title 6.27 Revised Code of Washington:

http://app.leg.wa.gov/rcw/default.aspx?cite=6.27

Washington Court Forms—Garnishment:

https://www.courts.wa.gov/forms/?fa=forms.contribute&formID=20

Washington Attorney General's Office—Garnishment & Other Withholding Documents: Processing Procedures:

www.wasbo.org/resource/resmgr/imported/Garnishment%20Procedures.pdf

ACKNOWLEDGEMENTS

The practice of law is just that: practice. A lawyer who professes to know everything is poor counsel. It is a process, an evolution, not a bank of absolute knowledge. Accordingly, I must give thanks to the many clients who provided me with the opportunity to learn and practice on their cases; to opposing counsel who allowed me to learn and teach; and to my mentor, Kevin Hanchett, who permitted me to take on cases that were beyond my comfort level, confident that I knew what I was doing or would at least learn before I did too much damage.

Thanks also to Daniel Brown and Beth Harman for reviewing and editing the manuscript, and to Beth Harman for suffering my request that she model for photos for the book.

ABOUT THE AUTHOR

Jeff Smoot is an attorney, writer, and photographer residing in Seattle, Washington. He is a frequent blogger and lecturer on legal topics.

GARNISHMENT

www.ingramcontent.com/pod-product-compliance
Lightning Source LLC
Chambersburg PA
CBHW071321220526
45468CB00001B/456